Donna Scott Munroe
1-5-87

THIRD EYE PHILOSOPHY

Third Eye Philosophy

Essays in East-West Thought

TROY WILSON ORGAN

OHIO UNIVERSITY PRESS
ATHENS, OHIO   LONDON

Library of Congress Cataloging-in-Publication Data

Organ, Troy Wilson.
  Third eye philosophy

Includes bibliographical references and index.
1. Philosophy.   2. Philosophy, Hindu.   I. Title.
B73.074   1987   100   86-12597
ISBN 0-8214-0851-8

Contents

Preface

According to Hindu mythology Lord Śiva preserves the world by looking at it. But when his wife Pārvatī once stole from behind and playfully covered his eyes with her hands, the world did not pass out of existence because a third eye burst forth in the middle of his forehead. On another occasion Śiva by a glance with his third eye reduced to ashes Kāma, the god of love, for having aroused amorous desires in Pārvatī at an inopportune time. So the third eye of Śiva is both the eye of preservation and the eye of destruction. In India looking at something from a different point of view is called "seeing with the third eye."

Philosophy is like that—or at least it ought to be. Augustine, in the midst of an analysis of the nature of memory, abruptly asked, "What third view is there?"[1] And Plotinus advised, "You must close the eyes and call instead upon another vision which is to be waked within you, a vision, a birth-right of all, which few turn to use."[2]

I submit that human beings have three "eyes." The scientific eye looks out. The religious eye looks in. The philosophical eye looks at the looking. These essays record some of my efforts to think differently, to destroy error, and let *Saccidānanda* (Being-Truth-Value) shine forth.

T.W.O.

NOTES

1. *Confessions* 10. 16.
2. *Enneads* 1. 6. 8.

1. Oxymorons as Theological Symbols*

An oxymoron is a locution which produces an effect by means of what in ordinary language is a self-contradiction. The word *oxymoron*, which comes from the Greek *oxus* (sharp) and *mōros* (dull), is defined in *The Oxford English Dictionary* as "A rhetorical figure by which contradictory or incongruous terms are conjoined so as to give point to the statement or expression; an expression in its superficial or literal meaning self-contradictory or absurd, but involving a point." This definition correctly implies—although it does not explicitly state—that there are two classes of oxymorons: (1) those which link contradictions, e.g., unholy holiness, and (2) those which link contraries, e.g., passionate detachment. The oxymorons of contrariety may not be so arresting as the oxymorons of contradiction, but they can be very effective. For example, "cheerful indifference" and "rigorous moderation"[1] are far more arresting than "unmiraculous miracles"[2] and "fluted unfluted."[3]

I first became aware of oxymorons many years ago when my high school teacher of Latin informed our class on the opening day that our motto would be *Festina lente* (Make haste slowly). The maxim struck me forcibly, for I had already observed how often I accomplished little when I acted quickly. Forty years later my mind flashed back to that day when, upon asking the great Zen Buddhist D. T. Suzuki what he did when he faced a contradiction, I was informed, "I just plunge right through."

Sometimes an oxymoronic idea is not expressed oxymoronically because of the oddity of the expression. For example, Dylan Thomas wrote in the last stanza of "Do Not Go Gentle into That Good Night,"

---

*This essay in an abbreviated form appears in *The Christian Century*, November 1984, pp. 1128-30.

And you, my father, there on the sad height,
Curse, bless, me now with your fierce tears, I pray.

I believe that Thomas wrote "Curse, bless, . . ." rather than "Curse or bless . . ." or "Curse and bless . . ." because the agonies of the dying father and the grieving son were such that any paternal blessing would have been a curse, and any paternal curse would have been a blessing. Therefore, I submit that the oxymoron "Curse-bless . . ." would have been the most appropriate form, however strange the hyphenated term might seem to be.

The absurdity of oxymorons should not be minimized. Oxymorons violate the principle of thought and being which Aristotle called "the most certain of all principles."[4] This precept, known as "the law of non-contradiction," was stated succinctly by Aristotle as "the same attribute cannot at the same time belong and not belong to the same subject and in the same respect."[5] *A* cannot be both *B* and not *B*. Aristotle added that the validity of the law of non-contradiction can be demonstrated by asking one who thinks he rejects it to say something. If he says "A is B," then point out to him that in stating "A is B" he is denying "A is non-B," and thus his own statement assumes the principle he thinks he rejects. But the defender of oxymorons can point out that human beings sometimes have experiences which cannot be properly described in a logic of exclusion. One of the most obvious of these is the experience of love. The love relationship is so close to its opposite, namely, hatred, that it is designated by many psychiatrists as a love-hate relationship. The defender of oxymorons might also remind the traditional Western logician that the use of words to describe a referent which has an ontological status independent of the language system is but one of the many uses of words. Words may denote, but they may also analogize, create, and even reject a referent. That is why a seer in the *Brihadāranyaka Upanisad*[6] advised his pupil not to meditate upon the meaning of words, why the *Tao Teh Ching* begins with the observation that the reality which can be expressed linguistically is not The Reality, and why Zen masters warn not to trust anyone who talks about the Buddha.

Oxymorons emerge in many unexpected places. A well-known analgesic balm has an oxymoronic trade name—Icy Hot. In the

United States cigarette advertisements which encourage people to smoke must also oxymoronically contain this warning: "The Surgeon General has Determined That Cigarette Smoking is Dangerous to Your Health." The Supreme Court of the United States in an important decision on the race problem stated that Blacks must be integrated into American life "with all deliberate speed." Physicists, having discovered that electrons are both particlelike and wavelike, sometimes use the coined term "wave-icles." Erwin Schrödinger in a thought experiment has stated that if a cat were described as a quantum system there is a preobservation condition in which the cat is in a "live-dead" condition. Philosophers have used the term "omnijective" to designate a view which is both objective and subjective. Botanists sometimes refer to trees of the *populus, nyssa,* and *plantanus* families as "soft hardwoods" and to the celastrus vine as "bittersweet." Dog trainers refer to "serious playfulness" and "playful seriousness" in canine behavior. Psychologists use the term "passive-agressive behavior" to denote acts in which one person tries to manipulate another by refusing to coöperate unless the other acts as the manipulator wishes. Natalie Shainess in her book on feminine behavior with its oxymoronic title *Sweet Suffering*[7] distinguishes three kinds of behavior: sadistic, masochistic, and sadomasochistic. Zen masters speak of "effortless effort," and coaches advise long-distance runners to make an effort to run effortlessly. Christians refer oxymoronically to the "offspring of the Virgin's womb." Aristotle offers an interesting oxymoronic observation about human learning and action: "What we must learn before we do, we learn by doing."[8] Shakespeare piled oxymoron upon oxymoron in *Romeo and Juliet:*

> O heavy lightness! serious vanity!
> Mis-shapen chaos of well-seeming forms!
> Feather of lead, bright smoke, cold fire,
> sick health![9]

One of the classical oxymorons in literature is Voltaire's reference to "Epicurean pessimists." This is similar to Bertrand Russell's defense of "unyielding despair" as the only rational attitude to be taken toward the human condition. Plotinus made lavish use of oxymorons. He described the One in his system as "formless-form."[10] The One is "not merely present everywhere but in addition

3

is nowhere-present."[11] The One is "both present and not present; not present as not being circumscribed by anything; yet, as being utterly unattached, not inhibited from presence at any point."[12] Souls are "everywhere-nowhere."[13]

The cross is a common oxymoronic sign in many cultures. It symbolizes a convergence of powers, principles, and entities from which an emergent may be expected. Among some primitive tribes the cross was associated with the production of fire by the rubbing together of two sticks known as the male and the female stick. The *ankh* or anserated cross of the ancient Egyptians was a combination of the sign for activity and passivity. In Christianity the cross symbolizes the emergence of salvation from the death of the *deus-homo*. Others have thought of the cross as the harmonious-unharmonious meeting of action-passion, positivity-negativity, superiority-inferiority, life-death, and heaven-earth.[14]

Oxymorons are perhaps more widely used in the Orient than in the Occident. All lovers of Chinese food are aware of sweet-sour meats. Chih-t'ao, a seventeenth-century artist, described the preferred method of Chinese art as "the method of no-method." Buddhists are advised to desire the state of desirelessness, and Zen Buddhists speak of the *satori* experience as taking place in "a timeless moment." In the *Vimatakirti Sūtra,* a Mahāyāna Buddhist text, the Bodhisattva Manjushri, when asked about the nature of reality, replies with "a thunderous silence."

In India oxymorons proliferate. According to the Upaniṣadic view of the Brahman, Nirguṇa Brahman is not being or nonbeing, but being-nonbeing (*sat-asat*). The reality of nonbeing is often described as the reality of "the son of a barren woman." Śaṅkara in his commentaries on the *Upaniṣads* referred to "the knowability of the Unknowable" and to "the whole real-unreal course of ordinary life." According to Mysore Hiriyanna the Ātman is "known only to those who do not know it."[15] Nimbarka's form of Vedāntism is known as Dvaita-Advaita (Dualism-Nondualism) and Rāmānuja referred to his Vedāntism as *Bhedābheda* (Difference-Nondifference). R.C. Zaehner titled his Gifford Lectures of 1967-68 on Indian religions *Concordant Discord*. Mahatma Gandhi described himself as a "cruelly-kind husband." One of the most curious oxymorons in Hinduism is the androgynous conception of Śiva. Śiva is sometimes worshipped

4

as Ardhanārīśvara (Hermaphrodite Lord). The god is shown as male-female in sculpture or painting in which male elements are exhibited on the right side of the body and female elements on the left side.[16]

Sarasvatī, the chief wife of Brahmā, the post-Vedic god of creation, appears in the *Rig Veda* as Vāch, the personification of the uttered word. Vāch, as the primordial sound, is described as "the inaudible sound." Later Vāch was visually hypostasized as *bindu* (dot), i.e., as position without dimension. This thing-nonthing has been represented in a painting by the modern Indian artist S. H. Raza. Raza painted *bindu* as a dark circle dissected vertically and horizontally by two barely visible white lines. Theoretically the four sections of the dark circle are said to appear as white, yellow, red, and blue. In 1982 the Indian Postal Service reproduced this painting on a two-rupee stamp.

In the Mādhyamika school of Buddhist thought a key concept is expressed by the word *śūnyatā*. This term, which is commonly translated "emptiness," is used to express a condition in which there is no ontological substance in the process of becoming and no reality independent of a language system. *Śūnyatā* is an "emptiness" which is neither eternalism, i.e., absolute oneness, nor nihilism, i.e., absolute nothingness. It is religously more, but metaphysically less, than being or becoming. Oxymorons are so integral to the Mādhyamika that one of its chief scriptures—the *Prajñāparamitā*—asserts that because intuitive wisdom (*prajñā*) is unobtainable, therefore human beings should strive to attain it with all their powers.[17]

Frederick J. Streng in his study of the Mādhyamika distinguishes the "mystical structure" and the "intuitive structure" of religious apprehension. The latter provides meaning through combining concepts which the former would regard as logically inconsistent, e.g., that Absolute Reality be known as both "being" and "nonbeing," as "here" and "not here," and as "God" and "man."[18] My contention is that what Streng calls the "intuitive structure" of religious apprehension is not the conjunctive, but the oxymoronic, relationship. Hence, Absolute Reality should be known as "being-nonbeing," "here-not here," and "God-man."

According to Benjamin Walker *śūnyatā* represents "an experience of final Non-Beingness flashing forth through the state of natural

5

beingness which is our temporal human existence. It is not mere negation, but a Negation of negation that is an Existence-Being beyond existence and being."[19] But Walker confuses, rather than clarifies, when he adds, "It is best defined by negatives."[20] What Walker should have stated is that the universe as _śūnyatā_ is best expressed by the negation of oxymorons, e.g., "not being-nonbeing" or "not existence-nonexistence" or "not becoming-nonbecoming." The linguistic device for symbolizing Absolute Reality in the Mādhyamika philosophy is known as affirmation-negation (_asti-nasti_, literally yes-no). But even the specialists on Mādhyamika cannot grasp this; e.g., T.R.V. Murti in his exhaustive study of the Mādhyamika system writes, "The Real is transcendent to thought; it is non-dual . . . free from the duality of 'is' and 'not-is.'"[21] But Murti, thinking that the Mādhyamika seeks to be "free from the duality of _'is' and 'not-is'_" rather than from "the _duality_ of 'is' and 'not-is'" fails to see that Mādhyamika nonduality is the oxymoronic "'is'-'not-is'" rather than the negation of "is" and "not-is." Murti also says that Mādhyamika "uses the language of negation."[22] But again he errs because he does not realize the Mādhyamika negation is not the negation of "is" and the negation of "not-is," but the negation of coupling "is" and "not-is" into the oxymoron "'is'-'not-is.'" Absolute Reality is not that which is not existent, nor not nonexistent, nor not both existent and nonexistent, nor not neither existent nor nonexistent but that which is existent-nonexistent. Reality transcends both empirical existence and empirical nonexistence and also the rationality which contends that if X exists, then X does not also nonexist. According to the Mādhyamika system "'is'-'not-is'" is the perfect Buddhist middle position between "It is" and "It is not."

Zen meditation is the practical application of the Mādhyamika. The Zen masters commonly command their students after the preliminaries of taking the proper meditative position to "think the unthinkable" until they reach the state beyond thinking. This absolutely transcendent state is a sense of emptiness (_śūnyatā_). Nishitani Keiji has recently offered the following description: "Our actual experience is, in its very being-in-the-world, not-being-in-the-world, because it is not-being-in-the-world, it is being-in-the-world."[23]

Modern physicists use oxymorons to express the nature of reality, e.g., "space-time" and "matter-energy." Fritjof Capra in _The Tao of_

Physics prepares the way for "matter-antimatter," "evolution-devolution," "particles-antiparticles," "quarks-antiquarks," and "part-whole."

Christianity is the most oxymoronic of all religions in that it is centered on the *deus-homo*, the one described in the Definition of Chalcedon as "truly God and truly man." The Church councils explained this does not mean that the Christ was half-God and half-man, nor 100% God and 100% man. The formulation was an effort to find a position between the Monophysites, who stressed the divinity of the Christ, and the Nestorians, who stressed the humanity of the Christ. The creedal statement is a striking affirmation that divinity and humanity are nondestructive polarities. Karl Barth made this discovery in his personal theological pilgrimage. Whereas the early Barth insisted that God is "Wholly Other," the later Barth, as he admitted, turned the rudder "an angle of exactly 180 degrees."[24] In "The Christian Message and the New Humanism" which he gave in Geneva at the Recontres Internationales on September 1, 1949, he confessed, "God and man are one in Jesus Christ and Jesus is perfect God and perfect man. It is from this point of view that we regard men."[25] In *The Humanity of God* he offered a *Retraktation*, commenting, "What expressions we used—in part taken over and in part newly invented!—above all, the famous 'wholly other.'"[26] In this volume he also stated—with a curious reference to "wholly other"—that his eyes had been opened "to the fact that God might actually be wholly other than the God confined to the musty shell of the Christian religious self-consciousness."[27] He added, "It is precisely God's *deity* which, rightly understood, includes his *humanity*. . . . It is when we look at Jesus Christ that we know decisively that God's deity does not exclude but includes his *humanity*. . . . God requires no exclusion of humanity, no non-humanity, not to speak of inhumanity, in order to be truly God. . . . God in his deity is human."[28]

St. Augustine in *On the Trinity* states that in the Christ "the Divinity is not changed into the creature, so as to cease to be Divinity nor the creature into Divinity, so as to cease to be creature."[29] Some have regarded the Incarnation itself oxymoronically. For example, A.H. Armstrong said in a paper given before the Plotinus Society at Oxford, England, on November 23, 1956, "The sense of the Incarnation as something utterly unexpected and paradoxical, something which we could not possibly have conceived it if had not happened seems to me an essential part of Christian faith in the Incarnate Word."[30] I regard this assertion as almost a Marcion heresy inasmuch as it cuts Christianity from its roots in Jewish Messianic expectations. Moreover, it completely ignores the recurrent theme of incarnation in such concepts as *avatāra* in Hinduism and *bodhisattva* in Buddhism.

A different oxymoron was used by D. T. Suzuki in his command address to the Emperor of Japan on April 24, 1946, as part of the effort making the Japanese Imperium more democratic after World War II. He said on that occasion, "In Christianity God is transcendental immanence; in Buddhism God is conceived as immanently transcendental." Suzuki added, "I believe that because Buddhism emphasises its immanent conception of God its devotees should study its transcendentalism, and that Christianity would do well to emphasise God's immanence."[31]

Some very significant oxymorons are hidden in the Bible. For example, although Revelation 1:8a—*"Ego eimi to Alpha kai Omega"*— is translated "I am the Alpha and the Omega" (Revised Standard Version), it might be translated "I am the Alpha-Omega" or "I am the Beginning-End." The alternative translation is defensible because of the use of *kai* (and) in Koine. Writers and speakers of Koine appear to have used *kai* as a transition or hesitation word much as some modern Americans use "and-a," "really," "hey," "you know," "I mean," and "you know what I mean." Therefore, Revelation 1:8b may be translated "The Lord God, The Was-Is-Will-Be" rather than "The Lord God, who is, who was, and who is to come." This translation defines God as that transcendence within which time may be differentiated rather than as that being whose nature includes—and presumably is exhausted by—time-past, time-present, and time-future. In The Was-Is-Will-Be, temporal differentiations are irrelevant. God cannot be measured by past, present, and future, for in the Past-Present-Future there is no "past," no "present," and no "future."

A similar oxymoron is hidden in the *Bhagavad Gītā*. The Sanskrit text of *Bhagavad Gītā* 10:32—*"sarganam adir atas ca madhyam cai 'va 'ham"*—is usually translated "Of creatures I am the beginning, the

8

end, and also the middle." But an oxymoronic translation would be better: "Of creatures I am The Beginning-Middle-End." The justification for this translation is the fact that the previous chapter contains an oxymoronic statement: "All beings rest in Me . . . and yet beings do not rest in Me."[32] Moreover, *BG* 9:17 should be "I am Fire-Water," i.e., the integration of destructive dualities, rather than "I am the fire of offering, and I am the poured oblation."

The Gnostic texts discovered at Nag Hammadi (Egypt) in 1945 reveal the richness of the oxymoronic use of terms to designate the Deity. Many of these texts refer to God as the dyad, i.e., the Divine as masculofeminine—"The Great Male-Female Power."[33] A remarkable poem in the texts, titled "Thunder, Perfect Mind," is this soliloquy of a feminine divine power:

> I am the first and the last.
> I am the honored one and the scorned one.
> I am the whore and the holy one.
> I am the wife and the virgin.
> I am knowledge and ignorance.
> I am foolish and I am wise.[34]

A more accurate translation would be, "I am The First-Last, The Scorned-Honored One, The Holy Whore, and The Virgin Mother. I am The Way of Ignorant Knowledge, and I am The Way of Foolish Wisdom."

Augustine referred to God as "that simple multiplicity, or multiform simplicity."[35] God is the one who "ever works and yet is ever at rest."[36] The Christ will and will not judge,[37] the Christ's doctrine is and is not known,[38] and the Christ is in the form of a servant and also in the form of God.[39] Holy Scripture, according to Augustine, in order to make its message understood, purges the human mind of its logical categories by the use of "words drawn from any class of things really existing."[40] Thus it "suits itself to babes."[41] It frames "allurements for children from the things which are found in the creature."[42] Augustine mentioned two ways in which this is done. One is by taking words from corporeal things and using them for that which is incorporeal; e.g., the Psalmist pleads "Hide me under the shadow of Thy wings,"[43] when God had no wings—and hence there can be no shadow. Another is by using words suitable to human psychology,

9

but unsuitable when applied to deity, e.g., "I the Lord thy God am a jealous God."[44] Augustine pointed out that Scripture does not use words "to frame either figures of speech or enigmatic sayings from things which do not exist at all,"[45] but it sometimes "employs those things which are spoken properly of God and are not found in any creature,"[46]e.g., "I am that I am."

Irenaeus, in his effort to integrate Christian insights and Greek wisdom, backed into an oxymoron: the god who cannot suffer (*Deus impassibilis*) is the God who suffers (*Deus passibilis*). Gregory Thaumaturgus in the next century picked up the theme of "the Suffering of Him who cannot suffer," and in the twentieth century H. Crouzel, L. Abramowski, and B.R. Bransnett have also used the same oxymoronic expression.[47] Jurgen Moltmann creates a quasi-oxymoron when he writes, "If God is love he is at once the lover, the beloved and the love itself."[48] God is Beloved-Lover-Love. Could the Trinity symbol itself be the ultimate oxymoron—God is Father-Son-Holy Spirit? Moltmann, in maintaining that the Holy Spirit is the feminine principle of the godhead, adumbrates an even more striking oxymoron, viz., God is Father-Mother-Son.[49]

The Christian Scholastics, upon concluding that God cannot be defined positively, tried the way of negation (*via negativa*), i.e., God is that which negates attributes. God is infinite, timeless, unchangeable, sinless, and deathless. God is remote from the limitations of space, time, change, sin, and death. The way of negation defines God by *exclusion*. When the theologian denies that God is spatial, temporal, changeable, sinful, and mortal, the theologian also denies that God is human. God becomes the Wholly Other. God and man exclude each other. But the way of the oxymoron defines God by *inclusion*. God includes space, for God is finite-infinite; God includes time, for God is The Past-Present-Future; God includes change, for God is change-nonchange; God includes sin, for God is sin-redemption; God includes death, for God is mortality-immortality; and God includes man, for God is *deus-homo*. This is the view of God expressed by Deutero-Isaiah:

> I am the Lord, there is no other;
> I make the light, I create darkness,
> author alike of prosperity and trouble.
> I, the Lord, do all these things.[50]

Was not this the conception of God which stimulated Paul to sing praise to an Inclusive God: "For I am persuaded that neither death, nor life, nor angels, nor principalities, nor things present, nor things to come, nor power, nor height, nor depth, nor any other creature, shall be able to separate us from the love of God."[51] We cannot be separated from God, for God is that which includes all. Sin, suffering, and death itself are not beyond the Reality which we symbolize by "God."

If someone who has understood the argument thus far objects because a being symbolized by an oxymoron cannot exist, I reply as follows: You correctly grasp one of the values in the use of oxymorons as theological symbols. Does God exist? Keep in mind that the word *existence* comes from the Latin *ex-sistere* (to stand out from). Existence is the mode of being which consists in interaction with other things in a class. Does God interact with other gods? If God stands out from any thing, then God is not inclusive. An existent God must be a limited God—limited by all that is non-God. The traditional philosophical arguments for God—the cosmological, the teleological, and the ontological—err in that they argue for the existence, i.e., the limited reality, of an excluding God rather than for the unlimited reality of an including God.

The oxymoron as a symbol for God has another value: it reminds us that the word *God* is equivocal. The two fundamental uses of *God* are often confused. Eckhart distinguished *Gott* (God) and *Gottheit* (Godhead). Śaṅkara distinguishes Saguṇa Brahman (the Brahman with attributes) and Nirguṇa Brahman (the Brahman without attributes). Tillich distinguished *God* and "The God Beyond God" or "The Ground of Being." The distinctions made by Eckhart, Śaṅkara, and Tillich are distinctions between a symbol and what the symbol symbolizes. I submit that *god* be used as the symbol, and "The Divine" for the referent. Other possibilities for the referent would be "The Good" of Plato, "The One" of Plotinus, and *Saccidānanda* of Aurobindo. *God* as symbol is relevant and important for purposes of worship. "The Divine" as what the symbol *God* symbolizes is relevant and important when one wishes to refer as rationally as possible to the integration of Ultimate Reality and Ultimate Value. Confusions between *God* as symbol and "The Divine" as referent of the symbol can be ludicrous; e.g., "May God

11

bless you" is appropriate, but "May the Ground of Being bless you" is an absurd mixing of two universes of discourse.

Charles Wesley incorporated four oxymorons in one stanza of a hymn:

> Hear him, ye deaf; his praise, ye dumb,
> your loosened tongues employ;
> ye blind, behold your Saviour come;
> and leap, ye lame, for joy.

The American poet Gene Derwood made an interesting claim for theological oxymorons in his poem "With God Conversing":

> The gloomy silhouettes of wings we forged
> With reason reasonless, are now enlarged.

My contention is that especially in theological language we must recognize the difficult relationship of the word and the referent. Perhaps Christians ought to examine semantically such statements as "The Word is God." In talking about God it is well to remember with the Buddhists that words are "fingers which point to the moon." We should look at that to which words point rather than at the words. Oxymoronic expressions help us to "see ineffably that which is ineffable,"[52] and to say "things that cannot be uttered."[53] They may even, in the words of Deutero-Isaiah, help us find what we do not seek.[54] The understanding of The Divine which an affirmation is supposed to convey may be distorted by the affirmation, and the understanding may dawn like an *eklampsis* (sudden illumination), as Plato says in the *Seventh Epistle*, when the affirmation is coupled with the negation of the affirmation.

NOTES

1. A. H. Armstrong in "Plotinus's Doctrine of the Infinite and Its Significance for Christian Thought" (*The Downside Review*, vol. 73, January 1955), p. 58 refers to "the cheerful indifference of Socrates and the rigorous moderation of Aristotle."
2. W. O. Chadwick in *The Victorian Church* (London: A. and C. Black, 1966), vol. 1, p. 53 speaks of "unmiraculous miracles."

3. Scholars' classification of a certain type of arrowheads of the American Indians.
4. *Metaphysics* 1005 b 22.
5. *Ibid.*, 1005 b 19.
6. 4. 4. 21.
7. New York: Bobbs-Merrill, 1984.
8. *Metaphysics* 1049 b 29-32; *Nicomachean Ethics* 1103 a 32-34.
9. Act I, Scene 1.
10. *Enneads* 6. 7. 33.
11. *Ibid.*, 3. 9. 3.
12. *Ibid.*, 5. 5. 9.
13. *Ibid.*, 6. 4. 3.
14. See J. E. Cirlot, *A Dictionary of Symbols.* 2d ed. Herbert Read, trans. (London: Routledge and Kegan Paul, 1971), pp. 68-71.
15. *The Essentials of Indian Philosophy.* (London: George Allen and Unwin, 1932), p. 20.
16. Hermaphroditism was also found among the Greek gods; e.g., Lewis Richard Rarnell in *The Cults of the Greek States* (Oxford: Clarendon Press, 1896), vol. 2, p. 628, reports the following statement about a statue of Venus Barbata: "There is in Cyprus a statue of her bearded, but with a female dress, with the sceptre and the sign of the male nature, and they think that the same goddess is both male and female."
17. Sangharakshita, *A Survey of Buddhism.* (Bangalore: The Indian Institute of World Culture, 1957), p. 329.
18. *Emptiness.* (New York: Abingdon Press, 1967), p. 81.
19. *Hindu World.* (London: George Allen and Unwin, 1968), vol. 2, p. 453.
20. *Ibid.*
21. *The Central Philosophy of Buddhism.* (London: George Allen and Unwin, 1960), p. 208.
22. *Ibid.*, p. 331.
23. "Emptiness and History." *The Eastern Buddhist*, spring 1980, p. 10.
24. *The Humanity of God.* (London: Collins, 1961), p. 41.
25. Karl Barth, *Against the Stream.* (London and Southampton: Camelot Press, 1954), p. 186.
26. p. 42.
27. *Ibid.*, p. 40.
28. *Ibid.*, pp. 46, 49, 50, 55.
29. I. 7.
30. "Salvation, Plotinian and Christian." (*The Downside Review*, vol. 75, April 1957), p. 131.
31. *The Essence of Buddhism.* (London: The Buddhist Society, 1946), p. 31.

32. *Bhagavad Gītā* 9. 4. 5.
33. See Elaine Pagels, *The Gnostic Gospels*. (New York: Random House, 1981), p. 61.
34. *Ibid.*, p. 66.
35. *On the Trinity* 6. 4. See also 6. 6. In 7. 1. he designated God as "the Divine simplicity."
36. *Confessions* 13. 37.
37. *On the Trinity* 1. 12.
38. *Ibid.*
39. *Ibid.*, 1. 13.
40. *Ibid.*, 1. 1.
41. *Ibid.*
42. *Ibid.*
43. Psalms 17:8.
44. Exodus 20:5.
45. *On the Trinity* 1. 1.
46. *Ibid.*
47. See especially B. R. Brasnett, *The Sufferings of the Impossible God*. (London: S.P.C.K., 1928).
48. *The Trinity and the Kingdom*. Margaret Kohl, trans. (New York: Harper and Row, 1981), p. 57.
49. *Ibid.*
50. Isaiah 45:6b-7. The New English Bible.
51. Romans 8:38.
52. *On the Trinity* 1. 1.
53. *Ibid.*, 7. 4.
54. Isaiah 65:1.

2. Icons, Idols, Ideals

In this chapter I shall discuss entities that point to other entities and the entities to which the former point. I might call them *pointers* and *pointees,* but I'll settle for *concepts* and *things*—in spite of the fact that *things* connotes greater concreteness than I intend by the term. I distinguish three kinds of things: iconic, idolic, and idyllic. I relate these things to three kinds of concepts: iconic, idolic, and ideal. And I apply the three-fold classification to religious concepts, especially to the Christian doctrine of the Trinity.

There is possibly a third use of the adjective *iconic,* i.e., iconic things, iconic concepts, and iconic *ways.* For example, A. H. Armstrong has written that all faiths, pieties, and theologies are "iconic ways" to God.[1] However, I submit that to refer to iconic *ways* is but to indicate the soterial use of iconic things and iconic concepts.

The distinction between things and concepts is related to the distinction Plato and Plotinus made between the sensible world and the intelligible world.[2]

If I am accused of blurring the distinction between things and concepts, my "defence" is that I am a Platonic-Aristotelian. A Platonic Form is an ontological-epistemological entity—both an object and an object of thought, and the fundamental Aristotelian doctrine of substance (*ousia*) is a classification of things, of what makes things things, and of categories used when speaking about things.

Things are objects which stimulate the eye to see, the ear to hear, the nose to smell. There are three kinds of things: (1) things-qua-icons, (2) things-qua-idols, and (3) things-qua-idylls. Things-qua-icons and things-qua-idols are things-qua-images. The realities and meanings of things-qua-images are not exhausted in their existence. They point to realities and meanings beyond their own reality and meaning as existing things. But the two have different functions.

15

Things-qua-icons *present*. Things-qua-idols *represent*. Iconic things exist as icons, and they present something other than themselves. Idolic things exist as idols, and they represent something other than themselves. Things-qua-idylls neither present nor represent. They *are*. Their realities and meanings are exhausted in their existence. They are not things-qua-images. According to Plotinus, those who penetrate "the inner sanctuary" of the temple "leave behind the outer images."[3]

The word *icon* comes from the Greek *eikōn*. The word has been used, according to Liddell and Scott, for likeness, image, portrait, semblance, similitude, simile, representation, and figure. But I wish to use the word *icon* in this essay as it is used in the Eastern Orthodox churches. Unfortunately, even good encyclopedias and dictionaries are not helpful for this use of the term. An icon, according to the *Encyclopedia Britannica,* is "any image or portrait- figure . . . especially applied to the *representations* in the Eastern Church of sacred personages, which are either flat paintings or in very low relief, sculptured figures being forbidden."[4] The *Oxford Dictionary* defines *icon* in the Eastern Orthodox sense as "A *representation* of some sacred personage, in painting, bas-relief, or mosaic, itself regarded as sacred, and honoured with a relative worship or adoration."[5] The serious error in both definitions is the classification of icons as representations. This fails to take account of the centuries of argument between the Eastern and Western Christian Churches over presentation versus representation. As Leonid Ouspensky and Vladimer Lossky state,". . . the icon is not a representation of the Deity, but an indication of a given person in Divine Life."[6] To affirm that icons *represent* is to confuse icons and idols.

The leaders of the Christian Church at first opposed the use of icons. The Mosaic admonition against idolatry and the pagan worship of idols were conditioning factors. In the third century Eusebius said that although he had seen many icons of Jesus, Peter, and Paul, he did not approve of their use in worship.[7] Yet by this time Christians insisted there were two ways of divine revelation: (1) by "the Word of God" and (2) by "the Image of God." The former was a Christian adaptation of the Greek concept of Logos. This had been firmly established by the author of the Fourth Gospel. The latter had two forms. One was that according to the Hebrew myth of creation

16

man was made in the "image of God," and therefore every human being is a theophany. The other was that only Jesus was "the Image of God." He was a unique, complete, and final divine revelation. No one else could claim to be an Image of God.

Meanwhile the leaders of the Christian communities argued about the appropriateness of the use of things-qua-icons in worship. A verbal settlement reached in the Second Council of Nicaea (787) stated,". . . we define, with all care and exactitude, that the venerable and holy images are set up in just the same way as the figure of the precious and life-giving cross; painted images, and those in mosaic and those of other suitable material, in the holy churches of God, on holy vessels and vestaments, on walls and in pictures, in houses and by the roadsides; images of our Lord and God and Saviour Jesus Christ and of our undefiled Lady, the holy God-bearer, and of the honourable angels, and of all saintly and holy men. For the more continually these are observed by means of such representations, so much the more will the beholders be representations, so much the more will the beholders be aroused to recollect the originals and to long after them, and to pay to the images the tribute of an embrace and a reverence of honor, *not to pay to them the actual worship* which is according to our faith, and which is proper only to the divine nature: but as to the figure of the venerable and life-giving cross, and to the holy Gospels and the other sacred monuments, so to those images to accord the honor of incense and oblation of lights, as it has been the pious custom of antiquity. For the honor paid to the image passes to its original, and he that adores an image adores in it the person depicted thereby."[8] The statement of the Council also included the following: "Iconography is by no means an invention of painters but is . . . an established law and tradition of the Catholic Church." This was an expression of the fear that artists would not be content to assume subordinate roles in the Church. Musicians, actors, poets, painters, sculptors, architects, and dancers are still censored when they introduce innovations into Christendom. One of the most recent examples is that of a sculptor commissioned by the Cathedral of St. John the Divine (New York City) who made a crucifix in which the Christ is female.

Icons, despite their aesthetic appeal, are not regarded by Eastern Orthodox churches as works of art. The aim of icons is to assist in

17

worship, to teach doctrine, and "to feed" the Christian worshipper. The physical features of the saints portrayed in icons—halo, thin nose, small mouth, and large eyes—are said to "transfigure" the human state. An icon is "an external expression of the transfigured state of man."[9] An icon presents rather than represents the saint to the devotee. The full-faced direct approach of the image is favored. Profiles are usually of persons not yet sanctified, such as the wise men and the shepherds in nativity scenes. The relation between the physical icon of wood, plaster, or oil and the saint portrayed is symbolical. Never is the worshipper to think that the saint looked exactly as the saint is portrayed by the icon.

Unfortunately, the difference between icons and idols is often not clearly made. The *Encyclopedia Britannica* makes an important distinction between two kinds of images: some are "merely an image, picture, or representation of a higher being, and itself void of value or power," and others are thought to be "the tenement or vehicle of the god and [are] fraught with Divine influence."[10] The former are in this paper designated as icons, although—to repeat—icons are regarded as presentations rather than representations. The term "representation" connotes pictorial likeness, and this is to be avoided by iconographers. The latter I am calling "idols." According to A. H. Armstrong an idol is "a God-concept or symbol which we take for God and worship as God."[11]

An article in the *Hastings Encyclopedia of Religion and Ethics* stresses the vital functions of idols: "Generally speaking, we may include in the category of idols all images that open or close their eyes, gesticulate, utter oracles, move of their own free will, or converse with their worshippers."[12] My modification would be to add ". . . or are believed to show animate activities." The image of Athena in the Parthenon was an idol in that she was believed on occasion to speak to her worshippers. The image of Kali at Dakshineswar Temple in north Calcutta was idolatrized in 1856 when Ramakrishna reported "suddenly the blessed Mother revealed Herself to me."[13] He added, "I used to see Her smiling, talking, consoling, or teaching me in various ways. . . . I actually felt Her breath on my hand."[14] Ramakrishna prior to this experience was an iconolater of Kali. From 1856 until his death he was an idolater of Kali. The image of the Blessed Virgin at Fatima became an idol on July 13, 1917, when the image spoke.

The distinctions of images, icons, and idols are often blurred because of ignorance and/or carelessness of theologians. For example, Eugene TeSelle uses all three terms in one sentence, assuming they are synonymous: ". . . Posidonius had used this line of analysis to criticize the *idolatries* of Greek civic religion, arguing that *images* only 'decrease awe and increase terror,' and had suggested instead that the true *icon* is the whole physical universe."[15]

Icons are efforts to present the unpresentable, to show the unshowable, "to express that which cannot be expressed by human means,"[16] and therefore the iconographer is always a "failure."[17]

Members of the Orthodox Christian churches insist they do not *worship* icons. They "reverence or venerate them."[18] "When an Orthodox kisses an icon or prostrates before it, he is not guilty of idolatry. The icon is not an idol but a symbol; the veneration shown to images is directed, not towards stone, wood, and paint, but towards the person depicted."[19] In other words, the reverence shown to the saint presented by the icon is to the saint via icon, not to the saint via idol—a one-way, not a two-way, relationship. The icon does not respond to the one who reverences it. The idol is believed on occasion to respond to the idolater.

An idol is worshipped. The Greek word *eidōlon* from which the word *idol* is derived, has a variety of uses, many inseparable from *eidōn*: image, form, spectre, apparition, counterpart, phantom, imitation, fancy, and likeness. In classical Greek, the word *eidōlon* was used for images in water or in a mirror. In the Hebrew-Christian biblical tradition it took on the connotation of a fictitious divinity. But in the Hindu tradition another way of thinking prevails: e.g., some Kṛṣṇa idolaters worship by throwing water on the mirror image of the idol, thus preserving the paint. The rationale is that the mirror image equals the wooden image. Historians of religion might call this an instance of sympathetic magic. The idol worshiper assumes that the image is neither an icon of divinity nor the full, complete, and excluding presence of divinity. The thing-qua-idol stands between the thing-qua-thing which *is* and thing-qua-icon which *presents*. The idol *represents* divinity. Presentation is an inani-

19

mate function. But representation is an animate function. The icon is seen, but does not see. The icon-iconolater relationship is asymmetrical, like "parent of," "cause of," "north of," and "taller than." But the idol is believed both to be experienced and to experience. The idol-idolator relationship is symmetrical, like "sibling of," "beside," and "proximate to."

An idol, because of its representative role, demands an idolothyte from the idolater. An icon as presentative makes no demands from the iconolater. There is no "iconothyte." The icon's ontic status is completely presentative. It exists only to present. It does not partake of the reality to which it points.

In the introductory paragraph of this essay reference was made to three kinds of things: iconic, idolic, and idyllic. What are idyllic things? The Greek word *eidullion* is the diminutive of *eidos*, and *eidos* was the term Plato used to symbolize his perfect universals, i.e., Ideas or Forms, from which all reality, all knowledge, and all value stem. So, if *eidos* stands for a Great Form, *eidullion* stands for a little form. But what is a little form? A clarification may be found in Aristotle. One of the most telling of his many criticisms of the Platonic Forms was his claim that Plato used the Forms for two functions which presupposed contrary ontological statuses of the Forms. Forms, as used by Plato, said Aristotle, are sometimes ontological-epistemological and sometimes ontological-axiological. When used to designate the objects of knowledge, the Forms are universal; but when used as standards of perfection, the Forms are particulars.

Thus, triangle as a plane figure having 180 degrees in its interior angles is the universal triangle—or triangularity; but an individual triangle, when judged as good or bad, is judged, not against triangularity, but against an ideal triangle which can be called a "perfect particular." A perfect particular is a paradigm which individuals may approximate, but can never realize. The universal triangle is the Great Form—the *eidos*. The perfect particular—the *eidullion*—is the diminutive of the Great Form.

Plotinus spelled out the implications of this Aristotelian insight. According to him there are Rational Principles or Forms of universals, of particulars (i.e., kinds, classes, or species of things), and of individuals.[20] For example, there is the Form of Horseness by which a certain animal is known as a horse. Plato would say this animal partakes of, or imitates, the Form of Horseness. There is also the Form of a perfect horse by which the perfection of an individual horse can be judged. The perfection in this case is a perfection of its kind. And there is the Form of each individual horse, i.e., the Form of Pegasus, the Form of Man O' War, the Form of Dobbin. Forms of individuals are the idyllic things in the spectrum of iconic things, idolic things, and idyllic things. Perfection here is self-perfection, the fulfillment of individual possibilities. Each individual has its own determining pattern in the world of eternal Forms—the heaven of ontic and epistemic universals, of standards of perfection of classes, and of ideal models for individuals.

One of the improvements Aristotle made in the Platonism in which he was educated and from which he never withdrew was the recognition that nature is "inveterately individualistic."[21] It was Plotinus who worked out the details of this Aristotelian insight. According to him there are three kinds of perfection: universal, particular, and individual. An idyllic thing is the perfect individual-qua-individual. Only Dobbin can be Dobbin. Dobbin *is* Dobbin. Dobbin is *all* Dobbin, and all Dobbin *is* Dobbin. Dobbin is perfect with respect to the perfection appropriate to Dobbin. Each individual is a state, a condition, a being unlike any other in its uniqueness. Each individual is perfect with the perfection appropriate to itself. Each individual is a perfect instance of itself. Each individual is as good as can be expected of each individual—each being what it is. An introspective awareness of individual perfection is indicated in such statements as "I am not quite myself today." Falling short of one's ideal is a common experience. It might even have been described as the original sin of the self-aware animal. But correction is needed: idyllic perfection must not be confused with genetic or specific perfection. Rembrandt with a wart on his nose is an idyll of Rembrandt-with-a-wart-on-his-nose, but not of Rembrandt-as-a-man, or Rembrandt-as-an-animal, or Rembrandt-as-a-being. The perfection of the individual need not include the perfection of the species nor of the genus nor of Totality. An idyll is not an idol perfected. Each thing is good, but not all are equally good.[22] There is, according to Plotinus, a distinct archetype for each of the innumerable individual things. Forms are "limitless," and yet their limitlessness is "an

21

infinitude which has nothing to do with number or part."[23] Part is not particle. Everything that is a part must come to its full perfection—a perfection which includes all things, since to Whole belongs its parts.[24] Dobbin, in fully realizing his nature as Dobbin, also realizes the being and meaning of the ontological-axiological Form of the perfect Horse and also the ontological-epistemological Form of the universal Horse. Moreover, for Plotinus, the Forms are parts of the One. The One, the Good, the Whole is the "Beyond Being" which is as dependent upon the parts as the parts are dependent upon It. The Whole without parts, in the words of B. A. G. Fuller, would be a "superunitary, superintelligible, superexistential, ineffable, and unindividuated divine Nothingness."[25] Plotinus, in discussing the dependence of part on Whole, wrote, "A man as individual is not the whole man."[26] He added, "The Whole is not envious of an increase of beauty and value in the part, since the greater value of the part makes the Whole more beautiful."[27]

An illustration may help clarify the distinction of icon, idol, and idyll. In South India a few miles east of the city of Mysore there is a hill known as Chalmundi. On Chalmundi is a Hindu temple, and near the temple is a large statue of a recumbent Brahman bull. It is an image of a much-loved god named Nandi. This colorfully painted structure of stone and cement is an icon inasmuch as it presents to Hindu devotees the divinity. Occasionally a woman will walk to the huge image, touch it lovingly, and then crawl under the bent front leg of the resting figure. This is part of a ritual believed by Hindus to promote fertility. In this act the woman believes that the image is sufficiently animate to do something about her infertile condition. Her act idolifies the icon. But when I, a non-Hindu, look at this image, it is for me neither an icon nor an idol since it neither presents nor represents a deity to me. For me it is a curiosity, a work of art, an interesting illustration of what Indians can do with mortar and paint, an object which helps me understand Shaivism, a possible shelter from the blazing sun, an idyllic thing which realizes its status as Nandi on Chalmundi Hill.

I wish now to apply this threefold classification of things to the Christian doctrine of the Trinity. The Holy Spirit is usually symbolized iconically by a descending dove or by tongues of fire. The Son has many icons, e.g., the bread and wine of the Eucharist, a heart, a vine, a fish, a cross, and an anchor. Icons for the Father are not fixed. An old white-bearded man positioned in the clouds appears in many medieval paintings. Perhaps the best known icon of creation is the hand with extended forefinger in Michelangelo's "The Creation." A few artists have portrayed the Creator in the act of "settling the compass on the face of the deep." One may look into other religious traditions for icons of creation; e.g., in Hinduism there are the _linga_ (phallus), the _yoni_ (vulva), _maithuna_ (sexual congress), the sound of a drum, and the dance of Śiva. The pine cone was an icon of creation in the old Roman religion. The icons of the Trinity as a unit are rich and varied, e.g., combinations of three triangles, three circles, three fishes, three hares, three wreaths, three fans, the fleur-de-lis, and the shamrock. But the most interesting icons of the Trinity are the human ones, e.g., three men, a man with three heads, and a human head with three faces.[28]

The best example of the idolatrizing of an icon in Christianity; that is, the shifting of the asymmetrical relation of icon-iconolater to the symmetrical relation of idol-idolater, is perhaps the historical shift from the cross as icon to the crucifix as idol. In 691 the Council of Trullo made official the change from a simple cross to a cross with the figure of a man on it. This prepared the way for new attitudes. No one—as far as I know—worships the descending dove or the finger of the Creator, nor has anyone claimed that either dove or finger spoke to a devotee. The distinction between iconic images and idolic images was blurred by the English Puritans. Cromwell and his followers destroyed that which they regarded as tending to idolatry. Two instances suffice: (1) The huge stained glass window in Winchester Cathedral (England) was reinstalled after it had been smashed by the Puritans. (2) All the lovely small sculptures of the Virgin except one were beheaded by the Puritans in the maiden chapel of Ely Cathedral (England). An example of the anti-idolatry attitudes of the time is that of Archbishop Parker who in 1559 required every parson at his induction and twice yearly afterward to repeat, "I do utterly disallow . . . expressing God invisible in the form of an old man, or the Holy Ghost in the form of a dove."[29]

All three members of the Trinity have become idyllic things; that is, they have passed from the image status as either iconic thing or idolic thing to a status beyond images—in this case, persons. The icon of creation has become God the Father, the icon of redemption has become God the Son, and the icon of presence has become God the Holy Spirit. This has created a labyrinth of problems which can be examined only after consideration of three forms of concepts.

Therefore, we now move from the sensible world to the intelligible world, from the world of iconic things, idolic things, and idyllic things to the world of iconic concepts, idolic concepts, and ideal concepts. Iconic concepts present; idolic concepts represent; ideal concepts are. In other words, iconic and idolic concepts have epistemic connotations; ideal concepts have ontic connotations. Icons and idols point to things other than themselves; idylls and ideals signify only themselves.

Iconic theological concepts state in intellectual terms the nature and function of deity as deity is understood in a culture. In Hinduism the basic iconic concepts of deity are creation, preservation, and destruction. When these iconic concepts are idolified, creation becomes the god Brahmā, preservation the god Viṣṇu, and destruction the god Śiva. These are the Trimurti, the three forms of god. Although the Trimurti is sometimes called "The Hindu Trinity," the relationship to the Christian Trinity is quite remote. In fact, the Sanskrit word *deva*, which is customarily translated *god*, has by some scholars been translated *hero, superman,* and *angel.* The word *deva* is from the root *div* (shine). The Trimurti is known religiously as Īśvara (The Lord) and philosophically as Saguṇa Brahman (Reality with qualities). When the Hindu seeks to understand his faith—that is, when he seeks to transform the idolic concepts into ideal concepts— he reaches a stalemate. He realizes that Brahmā, Viṣṇu, the Trimurti, Īśvara, and Saguṇa Brahman are symbols of Reality. They are versions of ways in which his tradition tries to represent that which cannot be represented, to express the inexpressible, to say the unsayable, to show the unshowable, to think that which is beyond thought. The idolic concepts are the attempted representations of Reality, the *māyā* (illusion) of *Sat* (Being). Metaphors express the Hindu exasperation in trying to pass from idolic concepts to ideal concepts: the Trimurti is the rope which a traveler mistakes at twilight for a snake, the sky flower which is seen in a cloud formation, the son of a barren woman. The Reality of which the gods are idols is called Nirguṇa Brahman (the reality which has no qualities) or

Saccidānanda. The latter term is formed of the Sanskrit terms for being (*sat*), consciousness (*chit*), and value (*ānanda*). *Saccidānanda*, therefore, connotes the harmony of being, knowing, and valuing. This is not to be understood as a pantheistic union of beings, truths, and values, but as an integration of the source of being, the source of knowledge, and the source of value—that which *is* is good and knowable, that which *is good* is real and knowable, and that which *is knowable* is good and real. But as source or ground of being-truth-value *Saccidānanda* is not a being. It is being-ness, knowable-ness, and good-ness. *Saccidānanda* and *Nirguṇa Brahman* are words which do not have an existent referent. Brahman—I shall use this term hereafter for Nirguṇa Brahman—is not an *it* nor a *he* nor a *she*. *Brahman* connotes the Absolute or Totality, and as such cannot be known, since no knower can stand outside the Absolute in order to know the Absolute as an epistemological object. "Brahman" may be better understood not as God, the World, the Universe, Totality, the All, but as a condition of Reality, i.e., the integration of being-knowing-valuing. Hindu philosophers of the Vedāntic schools conclude that the only way to "know" Brahman is through the way of negation, i.e., *neti, neti* (not this and not that). Brahman negates all concepts. Therefore, the best description of Brahman is that which negates is, is not, is and is not, and neither is nor is not, and that which negates what is known, what is not known, and what is known and not known, and what is neither known nor not known, and that which negates what is valued, what is not valued, what is both valued and not valued, and what is neither valued nor not valued. But even this description is flawed, for Brahman is no "what." The "what" or "that" said to denote Brahman appears in the *Upaniṣads* in the mantric expression *tat tvam asi* ("That you are" or "That is what you are.") Brahman is *you*—not the individual *you* associated with an individual body but the *you* adumbrated in those rare moments when one feels an identity with spouse, child, friend, and neighbor. The individual self in Hinduism is called the *jīva,* and the universal self is *Ātman.* When the Hindu affirms his faith that *Ātman* equals Brahman, what he affirms is that he is Brahman *mutatis mutandis.* The necessary change that must be made in order to have the *Ātman*-is-Brahman discovery is the realization that all limits of the self are self-imposed. The *jīva* is the *Ātman* seen under the shrinking influence of *māyā.*

25

The movement from iconic concepts to idolic concepts to ideal concepts, which has been traced thus far in Hinduism, has been described by Ernst Cassirer as progress from "a realm of mere indeterminateness to the realm of true generality."[30] Cassirer states, "So, guided by language, the mythic mind finally reaches a point where it is no longer contented with the variety, abundance and concrete fullness of divine attributes [iconic concepts], but where it seeks to attain, through the unity of the word, the unity of the God-idea [idolic concepts] but even here man's mind does not rest content; beyond this unity, it strives for a concept of Being that is unlimited by any particular manifestation, and therefore not expressible in any word, not called by any name [ideal concepts]."[31]

The iconic concepts of the Trimurti—creation, preservation, destruction—call attention to a serious omission in the iconic concepts of the Trinity—creation, redemption, presence. Christians, by failing to place destruction in the Godhead, create for themselves a serious problem with the fact of death. Death and destruction are intrusions into the Christian's world. They challenge the omnipotence of God. The persistence of destruction has often—albeit unofficially—been accounted for by a cosmic principle of evil although no sanctioned Christian creed contains the credo "I believe in the Devil," the belief is a part of Christian folklore. Hindus, on the other hand, hold that birth and death, creation and destruction, are alike acts of God.

The Trinity has never been a satisfactory concept. Augustine's *On the Trinity* is "one of the ablest presentations of the doctrine in Christian literature."[32] Augustine did not formulate the doctrine; rather he attempted to understand that which the Council of Constantinople in 381 had fashioned, viz., "Three *hypostases* and one *ousia*." The early Church Fathers called the articles of faith propounded by the Councils *symbola*. Augustine, perhaps because of his training in rhetoric, set for himself the task of explaining what the *symbola* symbolized. In the language of this chapter the Councils fashioned the iconic concepts, the churches transmogrified the iconic concepts into idolic concepts, and Augustine sought to delineate the ideal concepts which the icons presented and the idols represented. Augustine grumbled throughout *On the Trinity.* "It is difficult to contemplate and fully to know the substance of God."[33] "I am compelled to pick my way through a hard and obscure subject."[34] "I have undertaken the task, by the bidding and help of the Lord my God, not so much of discoursing with authority respecting things I know already, as of learning those things by piously discoursing of them."[35] He pleaded that his readers would recognize "the wearisome difficulties of the task" and would "make allowance for those who err in the investigation of so deep a secret."[36] "When the question is asked, What three? human language labors altogether under great poverty of speech. The answer, however, is given, three 'persons,' not that it might be spoken, but that it might not be left unspoken."[37] "Which of us understands the Almighty Trinity? And yet which speaks not of It, if indeed it be It? Rare is the soul which, while it speaks of It, knows what it speaks of."[38] Augustine finally concluded that the Trinity is an "enigma."[39] He was so conscious of the unsatisfactory condition of the work and so weary of the task that, after apologizing to readers for writing so loquaciously, he ended with a prayer which he said is "better than an argument,"[40] asking God to be the copy editor who would separate truth and error: "O Lord, the One God, God the Trinity, whatever I have said in these books that is of Thine, may they acknowledge what are Thine; if anything of my own, may it be pardoned both by Thee and by those who are Thine."[41]

The idolic concept of the Trinity continues to baffle Christians. Cyril C. Richardson, a twentieth-century Christian theologian, observes, "No doctrine is so fundamental to the Christian faith and yet so difficult as that of the Trinity. It has been observed that by denying it one may be in danger of losing one's soul, while by trying to understand it one may be in danger of losing one's wits."[42] Jurgen Moltmann argues that the Trinity should be understood as three ways in which God experiences man, rather than as three ways man experiences God; that is, God suffers with us, God suffers from us, and God suffers for us.[43] Augustine, according to Eugene Portalié, tried twenty-two formulations of the Trinity.[44] According to David E. Jenkins, the current Bishop of York, the Trinity is an "icon" and should never have been made into a doctrine. Jenkins writes, "I put the word 'doctrine,' referring to the Trinity, into inverted commas because it is not a wholly suitable word for designating the status and nature of the human conceptual entity or composition which is

27

referred to as 'the Trinity'. . . . 'The Trinity'. . . is much more of a symbol or icon. . . . Thus 'the Trinity' stands, not for a doctrine but for a way of life which is related to God's life. To reduce 'the Trinity' to doctrine or to metaphysics is to shrink its significance in a deadly way. 'Deadly' is not too strong a term to use, for the insight symbolized and maintained by the icon of the Trinity, with its doctrinal and metaphysical implications, is nothing less than the confident discovery that the possibilities of men and women *are* the possibilities of God."[45] The Trinity, concludes Jenkins, is the symbol of the perfect society, and the three parts of the Trinity are "communion, communication, and true communism."[46]

Jenkins' humanistic and humanitarian concerns are like a breath of fresh air in a musty library; yet an iconic conceptual formulation and a consideration of the social melioristic implications of the Trinity cannot entirely eliminate the metaphysical aspects. The iconic concepts are idolatrized into theological idolic concepts of Father, Son, and Holy Spirit. Making, saving, and abiding become conceptual idols of a Creator, a Savior, and a Presence; and the three "persons" are not only worshipped but also assumed to denote beings that can and do respond in some living fashion to worshippers.

The question to be raised is this: Is there an ideal concept beyond the concept of theological idols? I think there is—and I think it is crucial in the understanding of religion. R. G. Collingwood has stated the situation admirably: "Religion affirms God as its object, and . . . this affirmation is a misunderstanding of its own true nature. For though religion expresses itself in terms which, taken literally, imply the objective existence of God, its meaning is only apprehended when we make up our mind to regard these expressions as metaphorical statements of something else, something which is never by religion actually stated in literal terms, though it is capable of being so stated."[47]

There is nothing wrong with idolic things and idolic concepts so long as one recognizes they are idols. It is when idols are taken for that which they represent that problems arise. God as idol is useful as long as the concept remains idolatrous; but when the idolic concept deserts the representative function and assumes an ideal conceptual function, then serious problems arise. When idols of a culture transcend the culture, absolutism displaces relativism, finality displaces tentativeness, universalism displaces provincialism. The God of one's tribe becomes the God of the cosmos. The classic example is that of the Jewish people who became convinced during the Babylonian exile that their tribal deity was the deity of all the nations and that Yahweh had laid upon them the obligation to make all peoples worship him. Later Christian arrogance with respect to the God of the Christians led them to the notion that there is no other name under heaven whereby men and women can be saved than the name of the Christ. Hence they felt a duty to convert the entire world. But the Messianic complex is dangerous to the health of mankind, whether it be that of Jews, Christians, Muslims, or Communists.

What is this ideal concept of which God is an idolic concept? I submit that Eckhart is a good place to begin. Eckhart in one of his sermons petitioned, "I pray God that he might quit me of god, for unconditioned being is above god and all distinctions."[48] He distinguished God (_Gott_) and Godhead (_Gottheit_): "God and Godhead are as different from each other as heaven and earth."[49] His prayer might be restated: "I trust that, holding to the ideal concept of Godhead, I shall be released from dependence upon an idolic concept of a god." Perhaps this is what W. B. Yeats meant by the line "Hatred of God may bring the soul to God" in his poem "Ribh Considers Christian Love Insufficient." Eckhart's further clarification of the _Gott-Gottheit_ distinction—"There is only unity in the godhead and there is nothing to talk about it. God acts. The Godhead does not."[50]—is strikingly similar to the first line of the _Tao Teh Ching:_ "The Tao that can be stated is not the Tao." Moreover, Eckhart's further statement, "The difference between God and the Godhead is the difference between action and non-action,"[51] is exactly what Lao Tzu said about the Tao: "_Wei wu wei_" (Acts without acting.)

What Eckhard called "_Gottheit_" and what Lao Tzu called "The Tao" is known as The Good in Plato's _Republic_, the One in Plotinus' _Enneads_, Nirguṇa Brahman in Advaita Vedāntism, and Dharmakaya in Mahāyāna Buddhism. Jacob Boehme spoke of the Groundless

29

(*Ungrund*), Emerson of the Oversoul, Rudolf Otto of the Numinous, Alfred North Whitehead of the Void, Pierre Teilhard de Chardin of the Omega Point, and Paul Tillich of the Ground of Being.

According to Tillich, "The divine beings and the Supreme Being, God, are representations of that which is ultimately referred to in the religious act. They are representations, for the unconditioned transcendent surpasses every possible conception of a being, including even the conception of a Supreme Being."[52] The theist, not sensing the representative character of the idolic concept, stays with his gods or God. But all forms of theism are forms of idolatry. The atheist, perceiving the "atheism immanent in the religious act,"[53] moves to the "Unconditioned,"[54] which, if objectified, slips back into the level of idolic concepts. As Tillich says, "It is the religious function of atheism ever to remind us that the religious act has to do with the unconditioned transcendent."[55] Tillich thinks that the word *God* needs reinstatement so it will be equivalent to what I call "ideal concepts"; e.g., "The idea of God has, by misuse through objectification, lost its symbolic power in such measure that it serves largely as a concealment of the unconditioned transcendent rather than as a symbol for it."[56] I do not agree. The concept of God is quite adequate as an idolic concept for that which lies beyond all symbolization. One must, in the words of Eckhart, "Break the shell to get to the kernel."[57]

The ideal concept has no existence because it is not a being, has no value because it cannot value or be valued, and is unknowable because nothing can be external to it as knower. No thing can be external to the All to see the All as existent, as known, or as valuable. God is an idol. Father, Son, and Holy Spirit are idolets. They are idol and idolets of the ideal concept. Making, saving, and abiding are icons of the Ground of Being-Knowing-Valuing. The Absolute, the Totality, the Whole, the All, the One—or whatever name one chooses to use for the Nameless that is no name, for the Thatness that is no that, for the Goodness that is no good—is the ideal concept which idolic concepts in religions represent and iconic concepts in religions present. The good life—the examined life—the life that sees with the third eye—is the life of the iconolater-iconoclast who is also idolater-idoloclast. This is the one who revers the icons—both images and concepts, and worships the idols, both images and concepts, knowing they are icons and idols of that which cannot be iconized nor idolized. Faith in *Saccidānanda* is faith seeking understanding. *Crede ut intelligas.*

NOTES

1. "Negative Theology." (*The Downside Review,* vol. 95, 1977), p. 176, n. 1.
2. *Republic* 509D. *Enneads* 2. 4. 4; 3. 8. 11; 4. 8. 1; 5. 1. 4; 5. 3. 16.
3. *Enneads* 6. 9. 11.
4. 14th ed. vol. 12, p. 58. Italics are mine.
5. Italics are mine.
6. *The Meaning of Icons.* (Boston: Boston Book and Art Shop, 1952), p. 37.
7. *History of the Church,* 7:18.
8. *Documents of the Christian Church.* 2d ed. Selected and ed. by Henry Bettenson. (London: Oxford University Press, 1963), p. 130. Italics are mine.
9. Ouspensky and Lossky, *The Meaning of Icons,* p. 39.
10. 14th ed. vol. 12, p. 71.
11. "Negative Theology," p. 188.
12. Vol. 7, p. 116.
13. *Life of Ramakrishna.* Eighth Impression. (Calcutta: Advaita Ashrama, 1964), p. 71.
14. *Ibid.,* pp. 72, 75.
15. *Augustine the Theologian.* (London: Burns and Oates, 1970), p. 248. Italics are mine.
16. Ouspensky and Lossky, *The Meaning of Icons,* p. 49.
17. *Ibid.,* p. 50. R.G. Collingwood said this is true of all artists: "The artist's life is one of singular instability; it overreaches itself, bursts its own bonds, fails him at every turn." *Speculum Mentis.* (Oxford: Clarendon Press, 1924), p. 81.
18. Timothy Ware, *The Orthodox Church.* (Harmondsworth: Penquin, 1975), p. 40.
19. *Ibid.*
20. See *Enneads* 5:7. The issue of what Plotinus held is not certain. For analysis of this issue the student is advised to examine H.J. Blumenthal, "Did Plotinus Believe in Ideas of Individuals?" (*Phronesis,* vol. 14, 1969), pp. 77-96, John M. Rist, "Forms of Individuals in Plotinus" (*Classical Quarterly,* New Series, vol. 13, 1963), pp. 223-231, and A.H. Armstrong, "Form, Individual and Person in Plotinus" (*Dionysius,* vol. 1, 1977), pp. 49-68.

21. B. A. G. Fuller, *The Problem of Evil in Plotinus*. (Cambridge: Cambridge University Press, 1912), p. 92.
22. See *Enneads* 2. 9. 13.
23. *Ibid.*, 5. 7. 1.
24. *Ibid.*, 3. 2. 14.
25. *The Problem of Evil in Plotinus*, p. 140.
26. *Enneads* 3. 2. 14.
27. *Ibid.*
28. A three-faced icon of the Trinity may be seen in the chapter house of Salisbury Cathedral (England), although the person who wrote the guidebook to the chapter house was unaware that it symbolized the Trinity. Another three-faced icon is located in the Elgin Museum (Scotland). This is a cast made in 1832 by an Italian artist named Piccioni of an image carved on the newel of the stairway of the Bishop's Town House in Elgin in 1557. A three-faced icon has been carved under the organ on the rood screen of Yorkminster Cathedral (England). Also in York two fascinating images of the Trinity appear in the center panel of the east window of Holy Trinity Church, a thirteenth century edifice. In this window are two iconic presentations of the Trinity. In the upper part of the window the Father is a bearded man with nimbus who holds the nude body of the Son. The Holy Spirit appears as a descending dove. In the lower part of the window the Trinity is presented as three identical bearded men. This fascinating icon has been described as follows: "The three persons are all shown under human form. They are seated on one throne, and wear but one mantle between (*sic*) them, the ample folds of which lie across the knees of all three. The mantle is maroon lined with ermine, but the Holy Ghost has a blue under-robe. The right hand of the second and the third persons are (*sic*) raised in the act of blessing, and with the left they have evidently originally sup-ported the crown beneath, whilst it was being held above by the Eternal Father. All three Persons are shown as of one age, and wear arched or imperial crowns, the only distinction between (*sic*) them being in the figure of the Christ whose crown is enriched with thorns. His body is nude and shows the mark of scourging. In front of the Trinity the B.V. [Blessed Virgin] is seated with hands joined in prayer facing the spec-tator. Her hair hangs down her back as far as the waist. The head is an insertion and does not belong to the figure. On the left of the Virgin's head is a hand, but whether it belongs to the first or second Person is doubtful. It is possibly misplaced." (John A. Knowles, "The East Window of Holy Trinity Church, Goodramgate, York." *The Yorkshire Archaelogical Journal*, vol. 28, 1926, pp. 3-4.) Knowles does not note that

including the Virgin in the icon almost turns Trinity into Quadrinity. Similar Quadrinities appear in the Doddiscombsleigh Church in Devan and in a fifteenth century painting in the Basel Museum titled "Die Krönung Mariae durck die Dreieinigheit." In the latter the Virgin is shown being crowned by the Holy Trinity as the ultimate fulfillment of the drama of creation. God the Father is wearing a crown. God the Son and God the Holy Spirit do not have crowns. The Father is an old man with full white beard. The Son and the Holy Spirit have long dark hair. The difference in ages of the persons of the Trinity reflects the Arian controversy within Christianity.

29. Edward Cardwell. *Documentary Annals of the Reformed Church of England*, vol. 1. (Oxford: Oxford University Press, 1839), p. 234.
30. *Language and Myth.* Trans. by Susanne Langer. (New York and London: Harper, 1946), p. 74.
31. *Ibid.*, p. 73.
32. Cyril C. Richardson, "The Enigma of the Trinity" in *A Companion to the Study of St. Augustine*, ed. by Roy W. Battenhouse. (New York: Oxford University Press, 1955), p. 235.
33. *On the Trinity* 1. 1.
34. *Ibid.*, 1. 3.
35. *Ibid.*, 1. 5.
36. *Ibid.*, 2. 1.
37. *Ibid.*, 5. 9.
38. *Ibid.*, 13. 11.
39. *Ibid.*, 15. 1. 3.
40. *Ibid.*, 15. 27.
41. *Ibid.*, 15. 28.
42. "The Enigma of the Trinity," p. 235. As evidence, consider that Augustine said we use the word *persons*, but we do not mean persons, and Aquinas said we say *three*, but we do not mean three! A. B. Sharpe writes that "according to St. Thomas, the three Divine Persons are not three, nor the Divine unity one, in the ordinary sense, but only transcendentally; that is, they add nothing to the essential divine unity." ("The Many and the One," *The Dublin Review*, vol. 187, 1930), p. 98.
43. *The Trinity and the Kingdom.* (New York: Harper and Row, 1980), p. 4.
44. *A Guide to the Thought of St. Augustine*, trans. by Ralph Bastran. (London: Burns and Oates, 1960), pp. 134-35. The twenty-two are the following:

	"Father"	"Son"	"Holy Spirit"	Location
1.	Supreme being	Highest wisdom	Greatest good	*City of God* 11. 28.
2.	True eternity	Eternal truth	Eternal and true charity	*Ibid.*
3.	Eternity	Truth	Will	*On the Trinity* 4. 1-2.

33

4. Eternity	Truth	Happiness	*Ibid.*
5. Eternity	Form	Use	*Ibid.*, 6. 10, 11.
6. Father	Image	Gift	*Ibid.*
7. Origin of things	Beauty	Delight	*Ibid.*
8. Unity	Form	Order	*Ibid.*
9. Existence	Knowledge	Love of both	*City of God* 11. 27.
10. Being	Knowing	Willing	*Confessions* 13. 11, 12.
11. Being	Having form	Following law	*City of God* 11. 28.
12. Source of things	Distinction	Harmony	*On Diverse Questions* 83. 18.
13. Cause of being	Cause of kind of being	Cause of goodness of being	*Ibid.*
14. Nature	Education	Practice	*City of God* 11. 25.
15. Physics	Logic	Ethics	*Ibid.*
16. Object seen	External vision	Attention of mind	*On the Trinity* 11. 2.
17. Memory	Internal vision	Will (volition)	*Ibid.*, 11. 3, 6.
18. Being	Understanding	Life	*Ibid.*, 6. 10, 11.
19. Mind	Knowledge	Love	*Ibid.*, 10. 3.
20. Memory	Understanding	Will	*Ibid.*, 10. 11, 17.
21. Ability	Learning	Use	*Ibid.*
22. Memory (about God)	Understanding (of God)	Love (of God)	*Ibid.*, 14. 12, 15.

45. *The Contradiction of Christianity.* (London: SCM Press, 1975), pp. 142-3.
46. *Ibid.*, p. 159.
47. *Speculum Mentis*, p. 264.
48. Raymond Blakney, *Meister Eckhart.* (New York and London: Harper, 1941), p. 231.
49. *Ibid.*, p. 225.
50. *Ibid.*, p. 226.
51. *Ibid.*
52. "The Religious Symbol" in *Myth and Symbol*, ed. by F. W. Dillistone, (London: S.P.C.K., 1966), p. 27.
53. *Ibid.*
54. *Ibid.*, p. 28.
55. *Ibid.*
56. *Ibid.*, p. 33.
57. Blakney, *Meister Eckhart*, p. 148.

3. Is God A What?*

I wish to begin by setting the context of our thinking with five quotations. The first is from John Scotus Erigena: "God does not know himself, what he is, because he is not a what; in a certain respect he is incomprehensible to himself and to every intellect."[1] The second is from Philo: "God is better than the Good, antecedent to the One, and cannot be discerned by any being, since God is apprehensible only to God."[2] The third comes from Martin Buber: "God is not an object beside objects and hence cannot be reached by renunciation of objects. God, indeed, is not the cosmos, but far less is he Being minus cosmos. He is not to be found by subtraction and not to be loved by reduction."[3] The fourth, which comes from Augustine, may be regarded as the text of these remarks: ". . . in God to be is the same as to be strong, or to be just, or to be wise."[4] The fifth has to do with the Buddhist conception of *anātman* (non-soul). It comes from a fifth century A.D. work known as the *Suttanipāta*: "I am not a Brahmin, rajah's son, or merchant. Nor am I any what. I fare in the world a sage, of no-thing, homeless, self completely gone out."

The question I am raising is in what sense existence, whatness, quiddity, or haecceity may be appropriately applied to deity. The answer I shall offer and defend is that existence may be applied to God in the context of devotion but not in an ontological context. The concept *God* is a symbol designed to function as an aid in the realization of the integration of reality and value. But when the symbol is given ontic status, it becomes a hindrance rather than a help in the spiritual life.

"What is God?" appears to be a simple question. Yet, as every

*This essay has appeared in altered forms in *Philosophy in Context*, Fall, 1978, pp. 30-36 and in the *Bulletin of the Ramakrishna Mission of Culture*, (Calcutta, India), vol. 34, October 1983, pp. 220-2.

student of logic knows, it is difficult to ask a simple question, that is, a question which does not predispose the answer. "What is God?" seems to imply that God is a what, a thing, an object. If so, God is a member of a class of objects with attributes which distinguish God from other members of the class. Such an answer violates the uniqueness, the infinitude, the absoluteness which Judaism, Christianity, and Islam hold to be essential to the deity as traditionally understood. So we are to conclude that the question is illegitimate and ought not to be asked?

The Westminster Assembly of Divines meeting from 1643 to 1649 first formed a confession of faith and then attempted to express the confession in a contemporary educational instrument—a catechism. Among the questions the Assembly set for the new catechism was "What is God?" But the members soon ran into difficulty in agreeing upon an answer. At last they sought divine guidance. The member selected to offer the prayer of petition began, "O Thou who art a spirit, infinite, eternal, and unchangeable in Thy being, wisdom, power, holiness, justice, goodness, and truth." The members decided that the salutation was itself the answer to the question, and so they wrote the familiar definition of God. According to the catechism, God is a spirit distinguished from other spirits in being infinitely, eternally, and unchangeably real, wise, powerful, holy, just, good, and true.

What are the alternatives to spirit as a class within which to place the Christian God? One is the class of gods. The members might have said that the object of Christian worship is a god, and they could have added that while the Christian god is a god, he differs from the gods of the Babylonians, the Egyptians, the Greeks, and the Romans. This, however, would have been an unbiblical statement. Both the Hebrew prophets and the authors of the New Testament insisted that their God was not to be classified among the gods of their neighbors. The prophets said the gods of the other peoples of the Fertile Crescent were but creations of men's imagination. The Christians held that the heathen gods were in fact devils and demons. Paul at Lycaonia called the Greek gods "vanities." He told the people of Ephesus that Diana was but an object made by silversmiths. And at Athens he advised the people to stop thinking of

God as a thing: ". . . we ought not to think that the Godhead is like unto gold, or silver, or stone, graven by art and man's device."[5]

Again the Divines might have defined God as a person among persons. If God is a person, of course he is not limited in intelligence, morality, and mortality, as are other persons. Since persons are the highest form of life known to man, it is very tempting to classify God as a person or to insist that God cannot be less than personal. Christianity with its doctrine of the Trinity runs into curious problems, since each member of the Trinity is also a person. Then are there four persons—Father, Son, Holy Spirit, and God? Or are there three subpersons and one Person?[6]

The members of the Westminster Assembly avoided the problems of making the Christian God a god or a person. But the term "spirit" also has problems. Spirit may mean a ghost, a life principle, or enthusiastic loyalty. Some had defined God in terms of the spirit of goodwill, peace, and love. Santa Claus is the spirit of giving; Uncle Sam is the spirit of Americanism. God is the spirit of love, goodness, beauty, truth. But to define God is terms of "the spirit of" is not what is demanded in the question "What is God?" In at least one place in the Bible God is identified as a spirit,[7] while in many places references are made to "the spirit of God."[8] In defining God as a spirit rather than as the spirit of specific lofty ideals, the Divines were indicating their conviction that God indeed is a what.

Paul Tillich said that the question "What is God?" forces us into "supranaturalism"; that is, we agree that there are natural beings, such as trees, houses, butterflies, rocks, and human beings, and there is at least one supranatural being, namely, God. There are two undesirable results from this style of thinking. One is to create what we call negative theology. If God is a being, then he is a sort of thing very different from other beings. They are finite; he is infinite. They change; he is changeless. They are mortal; he is immortal. They are evil; he has no evil.

God as a being becomes wholly other than man. And that, of course, is the way Rudolf Otto thought of God—God is the Wholly Other. While there is much that is valuable in this way of thinking about God, Christians may rightly puzzle over a God in whose image man is said to be made, and yet who is wholly other than man. The second result which follows from thinking of God as a what is that we come to realize the terms we use to describe things cannot be applied in the same way to God-as-a-being and to beings-other-than-God. God is said to see, to hear, to know, and to love; and man is also said to see, to hear, to know, and to love. But surely these activities are not the same. Man needs eyes, ears, a brain, and other physical organs for these activities. Does God? Both God and man are said to be angry, jealous, and fearful, but not in the same manner or the same way. So theologians have defended what is called the language of analogy. God is a "father," yet not a father in the human sense. God is a "person," yet not like a human person. The problem is that we use a term which we understand when it applies to man, but we drain away all its meaning when it is applied to the deity. So we find ourselves using fine sounding words, but we are saying nothing. The language of analogy deteriorates into pious agnosticism.

The problem presented by the question "What is God?" is that it seems to predispose an answer which affirms God to be an entity in a class of entities, and this does not fit the transcendent qualities which theistic religions prefer to assign to the deity.

Augustine, almost as if he had anticipated the Westminster definition of God, wrote in *On the Trinity* Book 15, chap. 5, "If we say eternal, immortal, incorruptible, unchangeable, living, wise, powerful, beautiful, righteous, good, blessed, spirit; only the last of this list as it were seems to signify substance, but the rest to signify qualities of that substance; but it is not so in that ineffable and simple nature. For whatever seems to be predicated therein according to quality, is to be understood according to substance or essence. For far be it from us to predicate spirit of God according to substance and good according to quality; but both according to substance."[9] Each of the apparent qualities is a substance. So God, according to Augustine, is eternity, immortality, incorruptibility, unchangeableness, life, wisdom, power, beauty, righteousness, goodness, blessedness, and spirituality. There is no word expressing substance, nature, essence, and species, which can be stated as a class of which God is a member. There is no class of things to which God belongs. The Christian God is not a spirit nor a person nor even a god. In other passages in this treatise Augustine made similar observations. "God the Father is not wise, being wisdom itself."[10] God is "the essence of the truth itself."[11]

God is "the good itself."[12] God is "not a good mind, or a good angel, or the good heaven, but the good good."[13] God is "not good by a good that is other than Himself, but the good of all good."[14] "He is good without participation of any other good, because He Himself is the good by which He is good."[15] "God, therefore, does not live, unless by the life which He is to Himself."[16] Can man discern God? Augustine answers with a "Yes and No." For "if thou canst discern the good in itself, thou will have discerned God."[17] "God, not good by a good that is other than Himself, but the good of all good."[18] "It is not one thing for God to be, and another to be great or to be good."[19] "But in God to be is the same as to be strong, or to be just, or to be wise, or whatever is said of that simple multiplicity, or multifold simplicity, whereby to signify His substance."[20]

In *The Confessions* Augustine said that God "is not only good, but goodness itself."[21] Good is that which God wills, but in addition God "Himself is that good."[22] God is "the Good, needing no good";[23] that is, God as the Good is not ontologically or axiologically dependent upon exemplifications of Itself. God is "the whole, true, chief, and infinite Good."[24] In his treatise entitled *Concerning the Nature of Good* he wrote, "The highest good, than which there is no higher, is God. . . . He is the unchangeable good."[25] In *The Confessions* God is also described as the reification of truth: "For where I found truth, there I found my God, who is the Truth itself."[26] "O Eternal Truth . . . Thou art my God."[27]

Augustine as a Christian Platonist held that values are self-existent. The Good, the Beautiful, and the True are beyond being. They are not rooted in being. They do not, need not, and cannot in the final analysis be dependent upon anything for their reality. The destruction of all objects that are good and beautiful does not destroy Goodness and Beauty. God is Reality, Truth, Wisdom, and Beauty. The term *God* connotes the essential objectivity of values. One of his clearest statements of this appears in a discussion of the Incarnation: "For it is not, as with the creature, so with the Son of God before the incarnation and before He took upon Him our flesh, the Only-begotten by whom all things were made; that He *is* one thing, and *has* another: but He *is* in such a way as to *be* what He *has*. And this is said more plainly, if any one is fit to receive it, in that place where He says: 'For as the Father hath life in Himself, so hath He given to the Son to

39

have life in Himself.' For He did not give to Him, a ready existing and not having life, that He should have life in Himself; inasmuch as in that He is, He is life."[28] In Letter 137 Augustine offered another argument for God's non-existence: "He is able to be entire everywhere, and to be contained in no place. He is able to come without moving from the place where He was, and to go without leaving the spot from whence He came." God is not a being that *has* life, love, and existence. Man *has* life. God *is* life. Man *has* wisdom. God *is* wisdom. Man *has* love. God *is* love. Man *has* existence. God *is* existence. Augustine's Platonic profundity with respect to the reality of God is sometimes missed by commentators; e.g., Etienne Gilson once claimed that "to Augustine . . . proving the existence of God seems such a simple matter that it is scarcely worth bothering about."[29]

Paul Tillich objected to the Platonic view of values. He wrote, "If values have no *fundamentum in re* (cf. Plato's identification of the good with the essential structure, the ideas of being), they float in the air of a transcendent validity, or else they are subjected to pragmatic tests which are arbitrary and accidental unless they introduce an ontology of essences surreptitiously."[30] Tillich accused Plato and Augustine of having a theory of values with no foundation in reality. Tillich himself avoided the error made by the Westminster Divines—the error of making God a being among beings—by holding that God is the ground of being; but in his opposition to what he took to be the ontological weakness of Plato and Augustine, he tended to make values subjective. His term for religious values—"ultimate concern"—he defined as "What concerns us ultimately."[31] It is surprising to note how separate are his discussions of the ground of being and ultimate concerns. If Augustine made God values without an ontological foundation, Tillich made God ontological without sufficient emphasis on the values inherent in God. Both avoided the Westminster error of making God a what, but Augustine made God values detached from reality and Tillich made God reality detached from values. Both appear to imply that the question "What is God?" ought not to be asked, since for both of them God is the Absolute.

My contention is that the ancient *Upaniṣads* of India as interpreted by the Advaita Vedāntists offer a solution which justifies the question "What is God?" and avoids the problems inherent in the Augustinian and Tillichian conceptions of God. According to Advaita

Vedāntism—which I shall hereafter refer to as Vedāntism—the ground of all beings and all values is the Brahman. Brahman is not a god. The term is synonymous with the Absolute or Totality. All things and all values are manifestations or appearances of Brahman. Brahman is the All, the One without a second. Brahman cannot be known nor worshipped for the simple reason that knowing and worshipping require a distinction between knower and known, between worshipper and the object of worship. But no subject-object relationship can be established with respect to Brahman. There is nothing outside Brahman. Brahman is both knower and known, both worshipper and worshipped.

Brahman has no qualities. There Brahman is said to be qualityless (*nirguṇa*). This is what Augustine meant when he said God cannot be a substance with attributes. Brahman is the whatness of whats, the beingness of beings, the objectivity of objects, and the subjectivity of subjects. Vedāntists realize that, since Brahman is the All, everything affirmed of Brahman must also be denied of Brahman. Nothing can be excluded from Brahman. Brahman is, Brahman is not, Brahman both is and is not, Brahman neither is nor is not! The way of affirmation-negation must be carried to this extreme if one is to discuss the nature of Brahman. But this violates the law of noncontradiction, the fundamental law of all thought. Brahman reduces all speech to silence, all thought to no thought, all worship to no worship. Yet the seers of the *Upaniṣads* and the Vedāntic interpreters did in fact write and speak about Brahman. How can this be? The answer is that there are two modes of dealing with Brahman: *nirguṇa* (without qualities) and *saguṇa* (with qualities). Although the *Upaniṣads* refer to both Nirguṇa Brahman and Saguṇa Brahman, there is only one Brahman. *Nirguṇa* is Brahman as It is. *Saguṇa* is Brahman insofar as It can be talked about, thought about, and worshipped. *Nirguṇa* is Brahman in reality. *Saguṇa* is Brahman in appearance. *Nirguṇa* is Brahman as unknowable. *Saguṇa* is Brahman as knowable. *Nirguṇa* cannot be worshipped. *Saguṇa* is an object of worship. *Nirguṇa* is the Absolute. *Saguṇa* is Īśvara (The Lord). Both modes are legitimate. *Nirguṇa* presents Brahman as It is; *Saguṇa*, as It can be known.

A second insight of Vedāntism unites the axiology of Augustine and the ontology of Tillich. Augustine identified God as the Platonic

41

Form of the Good. Tillich defined God as the ground of being. But the Vedāntists refer to Nirguṇa Brahman as *Saccidānanda*. This is a composite term meaning being-consciousness-value. Brahman is the integration of reality and value. Vedāntism thus warns Augustine and Tillich against the separation of reality and value, and also against the notion that the Absolute can be an object of worship.

Vedāntism clarifies the problems inherent in the question "What is God?" by reminding us that the question is in the mode of religious worship, and therefore should not be answered as if it were a question about the Absolute. The Westminster Divines in declaring God to be a spirit were using the *saguṇa* mode; but when they defined the attributes as infinite, eternal, and unchangeable, they were affirming an absolutism. Augustine and Tillich, on the other hand, were discussing the Absolute, yet they both used the term *God*. Tillich said explicitly, "The being of God is being-itself. The being of God cannot be understood as the existence of being alongside others or above others. . . . Many confusions in the doctrine of God and many apologetic weaknesses could be avoided if God were understood first of all as being-itself or as the ground of being."[32] According to Vedāntism Tillich constantly confused his readers by referring to God as *The Ground of Being*. But this is the Absolute, not God. Vedāntism clarifies the issue by insisting that we carefully distinguish that denoted and designated by *Totality, The Absolute, The Ground of Being, Being-Itself, Nirguṇa Brahman,* and *Saccidānanda* and that denoted and designated by *Saguṇa Brahman, The Trimurti, The Lord,* and *God*. The former are in the mode of absolutism; the latter are in the mode of relativism.[33] The former are necessary for philosophy; the latter, for worship. "What is God?" is a proper question to ask when one is dealing with the ultimate object of worship, and the answer should refer to a being with qualities. But "What is God?" is not a proper question if one is asking about the Absolute. God is how reality must be limited in order to be worshipped. When Tillich wrote, "God does not exist. He is being-itself beyond essence and existence,"[34] and when Augustine denied that God is a substance, both were using *nirguṇa* language and should have used a term like *Brahman* rather than *God*. Being-itself does not exist; only concrete things exist. When the Westminster Divines sought to define God, they should have avoided *nirguṇa*-like absolutes. "What is God?" is a proper question in the framework of worship. "What is the Absolute?" is a metaphysical question which is basically unanswerable. God is an object of worship and is therefore a what. The Absolute is not a what and therefore cannot be an object of worship.

NOTES

1. Bertrand Russell, *A History of Western Philosophy*. (New York: Simon and Schuster, 1963), p. 405.
2. *De Praemiss et Poenis*, 40.
3. *Between Man and Man*. Trans. by Ronald Gregor Smith. (London: Collins, 1964), p. 80.
4. *On the Trinity* 6. 4.
5. Acts 17:29.
6. According to A. Hilary Armstrong ". . . to say firmly that it is literally and exactly true that God is a person in some understandable sense, and that our encounter with him is to be represented as an encounter of two persons, would seem to me to place him inside the totality of being as one particular among others, to make him a member, though no doubt the largest and most important member, of the cosmos, rather like Plotinus's World-Soul. If on the other hand we hold fast to the doctrine which has been accepted by very many Christians as well as by Neoplatonists that God is infinite and unknowable because absolutely undetermined and uncircumscribed, the Good who always lies over the edge of our thought so that it can only construct a multiplicity of inadequate images which may be means of his presence to us if we do not turn them into idols, but can never give a description of him; then we cannot say God is a person. We may still find it absolutely necessary, as Plotinus often does, to use personal language about our meeting with him. But in his own nature he is beyond our particular thinkings and particularities, even the ultimate particularity, at once most intimate and most capable of approximating to universality, which we call being a person or a self." "Form, Individual and Person in Plotinus" in *Plotinian and Christian Studies*. (London: Variorum Reprints, 1979), XX, pp. 67-8.
7. John 4:24.
8. Matthew 3:16; Romans 8:9; II Corinthians 3:3; Ephesians 4:30.
9. All quotations from *On the Trinity* are from the translation by A. W. Haddan.
10. *Ibid.*, 6. 1. Cf. ". . . the Father Himself is wisdom." (7. 1.); ". . . He is wisdom." (7. 2.) ". . . the Father is Himself wisdom." (7. 3.); ". . . the

43

Son is Wisdom of wisdom." (7 3.); " . . . He is Himself wisdom." (15. 5.); " . . . He is Himself His own wisdom." (15. 6.); " . . . the Wisdom which is God." (15. 6.) " . . . He is His own wisdom." (15. 7.)

11. *Ibid.,* 8. 2.
12. *Ibid.,* 8. 3.
13. *Ibid.*
14. *Ibid.* In this chapter Augustine also refers to God as "the unchangeable good," "the good in itself," and "the chief good."
15. Letter 153.
16. *On the Trinity* 15. 5.
17. *Ibid.,* 8. 3.
18. *Ibid.*
19. *Ibid.,* 6. 5. Cf. " . . . in Him it is not one thing to be blessed, and another to be great, or wise, or true, or good, or in a word to be Himself." (6. 7.); " . . . it is not one thing to Him to be great and another to be God." (7. 1.); " . . . it is not one thing to Him to be, and another to be great." (7. 1.); " . . . in the Trinity to be is the same as to be wise." (7. 4.); " . . . it is the same thing to Him to be God as to be." (7. 4.); " . . . to God it is not one thing to be, another to be a person, but it is absolutely the same thing." (7. 6.); " . . . to Him to be is the same as to be God, or to be great, or to be good." (7. 6.); " . . . to Him to be wise is to be." (15. 6.); " . . . to God to be is to be wise." (15. 7.)
20. *Ibid.,* 6. 4.
21. *Ibid.,* 7. 3. All quotations from *The Confessions* are from the translation of J. G. Pilkington.
22. *Ibid.,* 7. 4.
23. *Ibid.,* 13. 38.
24. *Ibid.,* 7. 5.
25. Chap. 1. Trans. by A. H. Newman.
26. 10. 24.
27. *Ibid.,* 7. 10.
28. *On the Trinity* 1. 12.
29. *The Christian Philosophy of Saint Augustine.* (London: Victor Gollancz, 1961), p. 11.
30. *Systematic Theology,* vol. 1. (Chicago: University of Chicago Press, 1951), p. 20.
31. *Ibid.,* p. 12.
32. *Ibid.,* p. 235. Tillich's desire to eliminate confusions in Christian theology was commendable, but he created new confusions in his strangely loose use of "the ground of being," "being-itself," and "the being of God."

33. Augustine was aware of this difference. He wrote that "the Trinity cannot in the same way be called the Father, except perhaps metaphorically." (*On the Trinity* 5. 11.) Also he wrote, "Position, and condition, and places and times are not said to be in God properly, but metaphorically." (*Ibid.*, 5. 8.)
34. *Systematic Theology*, vol. 1, p. 205.

4. True Deceivers

Wilbur M. Urban in *Language and Reality* asks, "Can we express truth in terms we know are not true?" He answers, "We have only to recognize that the question is wrongly stated, and to put it in its proper form, in order to get an immediate answer. We can, of course, express truth in terms which we know are not literally true, but not in terms that are wholly untrue."[1] But "literally true" and "wholly untrue" are puzzling terms—except perhaps in mathematics and formal logic. If one says he has "butterflies in his stomach," or "bats in his belfrey," or "a frog in his throat," or "a lion in his heart" is he speaking in a manner "wholly untrue"? Are these expressions "pictorially true" or "poetically true" or "psychologically true"? And how about religious truth?

Augustine in a letter to Jerome[2] criticized him for having stated in his commentary on Galatians 2:11-14 that in his opinion Paul, the author of the letter to the Galatians, wrote that Peter was wrong "in order to smooth troublesome opponents," when in fact Paul believed Peter was right. This, according to Augustine, could not be, for no author of Biblical statements deceives the reader. The Bible states only what is true.

Augustine, however, was sufficiently astute to recognize that biblical truth is not always patent. Therefore, he devised a four-fold methodology of biblical interpretation: (1) literal interpretation, (2) allegorical interpretation, (3) tropological interpretation, and (4) anagogical interpretation. Each interpretation was to be used with respect to a separate question: (1) What facts are narrated? (2) What things to come are foretold? (3) What is the reader admonished to do? (4) What eternal things are intimated?[3] Unfortunately, the Bible does not always indicate which interpretation is to be applied in the interpretation of a passage.

The Apostle Paul on one occasion advised that deception is sometimes required as a way of telling the truth.[4] During his second journey to Greece he had established a Christian Church in Corinth. Some of the members of this church were converts from Judaism; others were converts from Greek cults. The Jews were separating themselves from the *Torah*. The former cultists were separating themselves from idol worship. Both were having problems. Paul, upon learning of their troubles while he was on his third tour of Greece, wrote two letters to the church, one from Ephesus and one from Macedonia. These are preserved as "First Corinthians" and "Second Corinthians" in the New Testament.

The first letter was painful to write. Paul reports in the letter that he wrote with great anguish of heart and with many tears. Yet he expressed his confidence that the Corinthians could and would right the wrongs in their church and in their personal lives. He pleaded with them to stop bickering. The members of the church had divided into four parties. Some followed Paul; others said they were followers of Apollos; a third group regarded Peter as their authority and advisor; and a fourth party held that they followed only the Christ. The Jews in the Corinthian church were asking Paul to give them a divine sign to settle the issue, and the Greeks were asking Paul to display wisdom. In other words, half the church members wanted a religious miracle to settle the controversies, and the other half wanted a rational solution. It must have been a very interesting quarrel between those who regarded revelation as the final authority and those who trusted only reason.

Paul refused to satisfy either demand. He neither prayed for a sign from heaven nor argued like a philosopher. The vision he had received on his way to Damascus was the only proof he wanted. He had tried unsuccessfully the philosophical approach at Mars Hill in Athens during his first visit. What Paul preferred was to tell the story of a God-man—Jesus the Christ—who had been crucified at Jerusalem and had risen from the dead three days later. But the resurrection was regarded by Jews as "a stumbling block" and by Greeks as "foolishness." In his first letter Paul reminded them he had been very patient. He had given them a diet fit for children rather than adult food. His own words were "I have fed you with milk, and not with meat."

The Corinthians were also having problems in the sexual di-

47

mensions of life. At one point Paul became exasperated and wrote that they might be better off if no one married.[5] In another section of this fascinating letter he recommended that the women stop talking in church: "Let your women keep silence in the churches; for it is not permitted unto them to speak; but they are commanded to be under obedience, as also saith the law. And if they will learn any thing, let them ask their husbands at home: for it is a shame for women to speak in the church."[6] He even told the Corinthians how to cut their hair. Long hair is a "shame" for men and a "glory" for women.[7] But not all is puerile or picayunish in his letter. It also contains the magnificent panegyric to love: "Though I speak with the tongues of men and of angels, and have not love, I am become as sounding brass or a tinkling cymbal."[8]

Before the year was completed Paul wrote again to the Corinthians. Because he had become despondent about them after he left Ephesus, he wrote a second letter. The moral conditions at Corinth seem to have improved, but the factionalism had increased. Indeed, a new party had arisen which was openly hostile to Paul. In the second letter—a more restrained letter—Paul addressed one part to those who had remained faithful to him. He called them "ministers of God," and he advised them to be patient in the afflictions and hardships which had been heaped upon them. He referred to beatings, imprisonments, tumults, watchings, and fastings; and he warned them to wear an armour of righteousness on both the left and the right sides, for they would never know whether they would be attacked by liberals or by conservatives.

The dual attacks on the members of the pro-Pauline party were itemized by Paul as eight paradoxes:[9]

1. We are honored, yet we are dishonored.
2. We are accused of bearing an evil report, yet we are approved for bearing a good report.
3. We are said to be deceivers, yet we are praised for telling the truth.
4. We are unknown, yet we are well known.
5. We are dying, yet we are living.
6. We are sorrowful, yet we always rejoice.
7. We are poor, yet we are rich.
8. We have nothing, yet we possess all things.

Paul generalized that these are the paradoxes of the Christian life. There are two kinds of paradoxes: one asserts a seemingly contradictory situation; the other, an actually contradictory situation. Paul apparently had the former in mind. Augustine quotes this passage from Paul, complimenting his use of *antitheta* (opposites) and adding, "Paul used it with great charm."[10] The passage reminded Augustine that God made the world "like a fair poem, more gracious by antithetic figures" such as light and darkness, day and night, virtue and vice.

I submit that the eight are better classified as polarities or oxymorons than as paradoxes, opposites, or antitheses. They are duals that do not cancel each other. Their truth lies not in one or the other but in both. The eight are therefore better stated in this form:

1. We are an honored-dishonored people.
2. We are bearers of a good-evil report.
3. We are true-deceivers.
4. We are an unknown-known people.
5. We are living-dying.
6. We are engaged in sorrowing-rejoicing.
7. We are the impoverished-rich.
8. We are the nothing-everything possessors.

These oxymorons describe the paradigmatic life of the religious few who not only live a life which integrates reality and values but also are aware of the precious and precarious nature of that integration. The religious life avoids destructive dualisms—both the ontological and the axiological, i.e., both the view that bifurcates the world into the natural and the supernatural and the view which separates values into the material and the spiritual. Not "heaven and earth" but a "heavenly earth" and "earthly heaven." Not "transcendence and immanence" but "transcendent immanence" and "immanent transcendence." Not "time or eternity" but "time in eternity" and "eternity in time." Not "good or evil" but "good in evil" and "evil in good." Not "human or divine" but "divine humanity" and "human divinity." Not "God or man" but *deus-homo*. Not "truth or falsehood" but "deceptive truths" and "true deceptions."

This analysis is confined to the third oxymoron in Paul's list: "We are deceivers, yet we tell the truth."[11] Paul appears to have agreed with both those who accused the pro-Paulists of lying and those who defended the pro-Paulists as defenders of the truth. He asked them to identify themselves as "deceiving truth-tellers" or as "true deceivers." In extreme form this could be "true-liars" or "lying-truth-tellers." What did Paul mean by this strange claim about Christians? How can Christians be both deceivers and truth-tellers? An answer was adumbrated by Reinhold Niebuhr: "Among the paradoxes with which St. Paul describes the character, the vicissitudes and the faith of the Christian ministry, the phrase 'as deceivers yet true' is particularly intriguing. Following immediately after the phrase 'by evil report and good report' it probably defines the evil reports which were circulated about him as charges of deception and dishonesty. This charge is refuted with his 'yet true.' But the question arises as to why the charge is admitted before it is refuted. Perhaps this is done merely for the sake of preserving an unbroken line of paradoxical statements. If this be the case, a mere canon of rhetorical style has prompted a very profound statement. For what is true in the Christian religion can be expressed only in symbols which contain a certain degree of provisional and superficial deception. Every apologist of the Christian faith might well, therefore, make the Pauline phrase his own. We do teach the truth by deception. We are deceivers, yet true."[12] Niebuhr added, "The Christian religion may be characterized as one which has transmuted primitive religious and artistic myths and symbols without fully rationalizing them. . . . Every mythical idea contains a primitive deception and a more ultimate one."[13]

What Paul recognized and what Niebuhr stated is that religion is taught in symbols which contain a degree of deception. Religion is an abstraction. It cannot be seen, heard, felt, tasted, or smelled. If someone insists he has religion, he cannot appeal to any sense experience to verify the claim. Religion is an inner experience which may be pointed to by language symbols, but words are inadequate to express the meaning of the experience. Indeed, words can be very deceptive. Words must often be supplemented in ordinary conversation with gestures. I once asked a student in my class to stand before the class, to put his hands in his pockets, and to describe a spiral staircase. We laughed as he rotated his head to demonstrate what he meant by a spiral staircase. How much more difficult it is to express an inner experience. "How did you feel when you learned you had won $100,000 in the lottery?" asks a TV interviewer. What a ridiculous question! And what silly answers are usually given! The opening lines of a well-known book on Christian mysticism are "I feel! I feel! Oh, how I feel! I can't tell you how I feel!" Madame Guyon then wrote hundreds of pages to try to do what she said she could not do. Words, symbols, fables, stories, myths, and images are often used to describe the mystical experience. None is adequate. None is inadequate. A fable, said Jean de La Fontaine, "is a lie that tells the truth." Deception arises when the receiver confuses the symbol for the reality, i.e., when the receiver forgets the symbolic nature of religious language. The teacher of religion taken literally is a deceiver.

A few examples may help. Paul, along with the other Christians of his day, shared the book of Genesis. When one reads in the first chapters that God created the world in six days and rested on the seventh, and one takes this to mean that a world maker literally made this planet in six 24-hour days, one is being deceived. This ancient Hebrew story is not an alternative to geology or astronomy. It is a myth written among other reasons to support the notion of a day of rest every seventh day—a practice, by the way, which the Hebrews appear to have adopted from their Babylonian neighbors. While it is interesting to know that the Hebrew word translated *day* is the word *yom* which means any indefinite period of time, the problem is far from being solved by arguing that God created the universe in six eras. That is also a deception. The story is true only when it is understood as a symbolic way of saying that in some fashion realities are integral with values. To miss the symbolism is to trip over the words and to ignore the rich meaning.

Or take the classic example from the book of Jonah. Was there really a man named Jonah? Was he actually swallowed by a whale? To ask such questions is to be deceived, and to miss the truth. The truth behind the symbolic story is that man cannot escape the implications of his own sociality.

A third example gets to the center of the Christian message. Paul had much to say about the crucifixion of Jesus on the cross. Was God literally concentrated in one man so that when Jesus was crucified

51

God was entirely and completely on the cross? This literal view was later called the heresy of Patripassianism (Father Suffering). This was a literalization of the Pauline message. But Paul seems to have known better. God, the omnipresent and the eternal, was not concentrated in one place and one time. The truth is that the redemptive powers of totality—which can be designated as "God"—are always active and everywhere present. The crucifixion was a dramatic presentation of eternal healing, forgiving, and redeeming. But to teach this truth Paul expressed it in terms of the death of Jesus on the cross. When Christians later tried to explain the workings of this atonement, they used many different methods; some compared it to the ancient Hebrew sacrifice of a lamb for the sins of the tribe; others argued it was a ransom paid to the forces of evil; others said it was an effort to satisfy divine justice; and still others maintained it was a technique to influence the moral efforts of human beings. None has been agreed upon by the Christian Church. All the theories of atonement are defective and deceptive. As Niebuhr said, "This doctrine of the atoning death of the Son of God upon the cross has led to many theological errors, among them to theories of substitutionary atonement which outrage the moral sense."[14] The theories deceive, yet they truly hint at the central message of Christianity, viz., that values are inherent in reality.

The symbol of the Trinity is a classic example of a deception that is true. The Church officially arrived at the doctrine of the Trinity in the Second Council of Constantinople in 382. Between 400 and 416 Augustine, that great fountainead of Christian orthodoxy, wrote a careful treatise entitled *On the Trinity*. "I am compelled to pick my way through a hard and obscure subject," he wrote.[15] He regarded the Trinity as a dreary issue: "Since men weary us with asking such questions, e.g., how the Trinity uttered that voice which was only of the Father; and how the same Trinity created that flesh in which the Son only was born of the Virgin; and how the very same Trinity itself wrought that form of a dove, in which the Holy Spirit only appeared, let us unfold to them, as we are able, whatever wisdom God's gift has bestowed upon our weakness on this subject."[16]

Augustine did not feel authoritative on the subject. Hence he wrote, "I have undertaken the task . . . not so much of discoursing with authority respecting things I know already, as of learning those things by piously discoursing of them."[17] He seemed resigned to the doctrine because it had been made official by the Church, and not because he had arrived at the doctrine through his own efforts: "This is also my faith, since it is the Catholic Faith."[18] He pleaded that people ought "to make allowance for those who err in the investigation of so deep a secret."[19] He warned that some "will imagine that I have held sentiments which I have not held."[20] He added that "no man ever so spoke as to be understood in all things by all men."[21]

Again he wrote that "in no other subject is error more dangerous, or inquiry more laborious, or the discovery of truth more profitable."[22] As one reads this ponderous document, one may wonder why Augustine so frequently warned his readers against misunderstanding him. The answer, according to Augustine, is that the Bible "in speaking of God . . . has both used words taken from things corporeal, as when it says 'Hide me under the shadow of Thy wings'; and it has borrowed many things from the spiritual creature, whereby to signify that which indeed is not so, but needs to be said."[23] God does not have wings, they cannot cast a shadow, and we cannot be hidden under them. Yet the Bible tells us to pray God to hide us under His wings.

Augustine, after giving this warning, attempts to analyze the doctrine of the Trinity. God is not a being in three persons. The term "God" symbolizes being itself, goodness itself, and truth itself (*esse ipsum, bonum ipsum, verum ipsum*). Yet in a deceptive manner we say that God is three persons. "Father, Son, and Holy Spirit" is an appealing yet inadequate way to symbolize creation, redemption, and presence. The Trinity is deceptive if taken literally; it is true if taken symbolically. Even though Christendom has held to the creedal affirmation, the qualifications have been remarkable. For example, as A. B. Sharpe has written, "According to St. Thomas, the three Divine Persons are not three, nor the Divine Unity one, in the ordinary sense, but only transcendentally."[24] David E. Jenkins has stated that the "three persons" formula does not point to "person, personality, or personhood."[25] So the modern Christian reciting a Christian creed is to understand that although he says "three persons," he does not mean "three" nor "persons." If he seems confused, let him remember that even Paul admitted that in such matters we see through a mirror enigmatically.[26]

53

Hindus, when speaking of what their gods symbolize, sometimes use the expression *"Neti, neti"* (Not this, not that). This means that everything said is partially false, or obversely, nothing that can be said is completely true. The great wisdom in this observation is that the Divine cannot be literally described. Part of the reason for this is the fact that the Indo-European family of languages implies substances, things, and beings as referent of nouns. Hence, God-talk must be figurative, mythological, and suggestive if it is to be adequate. As Kant warned, the mind falls into antinomies when it tries to go beyond the world of temporal and spatial existence.

Theology is best understood as an art form. It uses myths, parables, and oxymorons. Theology deceives when interpreted literally, but it deceives truly when it is interpreted symbolically. Religious language fails when it succeeds, and succeeds when it fails.

NOTES

1. London: George Allen and Unwin, (1939), p. 593.
2. Letter 24.
3. *De Genesi ad Litteram Imperfectus Liberi.*
4. I Corinthians 3:2.
5. *Ibid.,* 7:7.
6. *Ibid.,* 14:34, 35.
7. *Ibid.,* 11:14, 15.
8. *Ibid.,* 13:1.
9. II Corinthians 6:7-10.
10. *The City of God* 2. 18.
11. II Corinthians 6:8b *"ōs planoi kai alētheis."*
12. *Beyond Tragedy.* (London: Nisbet, 1938), p. 3.
13. *Ibid.,* pp. 7, 9.
14. *Ibid.,* pp. 17-18.
15. *On the Trinity* 1. 5.
16. *Ibid.,* 1. 5.
17. *Ibid.*
18. *Ibid.,* 1. 4.
19. *Ibid.,* 2. 1.
20. *Ibid.,* 1. 3.
21. *Ibid.*
22. *Ibid.*
23. *Ibid.,* 1. 1.

24. "The Many and the One," *The Dublin Review*, vol. 187, (1930), p. 98.
25. *The Contradictions of Christianity.* (London: SCM Press, 1976), p. 153.
26. I Corinthians 13:12. The Greek term *ainigma* means an obscure analogy.

5. In Defense of Heresy

> By the light of burning heretics,
> Jesus' bleeding feet we track.

So wrote James Russell Lowell in his poem "The Present Crisis." But when portions of the poem were made into a hymn, the hymnist, obviously doubting that heretics could witness to the truths and values of Christianity, altered the poem to celebrate martyrs rather than heretics.

> By the light of burning martyrs,
> Christ, your bleeding feet we track.

The hymn extols those whom the world persecutes; the poem, those whom the church persecutes. The hymn version is much more acceptable to Christians. The intent of this study is to put the heretics back in the perspective Lowell intended. I seek to trace the light of the heretics.

What is heresy, and who are the heretics? The word itself is instructive. The Greek term *hairesis* originally meant a taking or conquering, especially the seizing of a town by military force. But the meaning shifted to indicate the taking for oneself, that is, the making of a choice. A heretic is one who prefers to make a personal choice rather than accept and support the view held by the majority of his community. A heretic is a nonconformer. His nonconformity is in the area of thought, although it is reflected in action. Heresy usually denotes aberrant beliefs in religion; but it can also refer to deviations in moral, economic, social, and political thinking. A heretic is a loner. The Greek term *hairesis* is curiously related to the term *idios* from which we derive the English word *idiot*. But an *idios* in classical Greek was not one with a low intelligence quotient. Rather an *idios* was one who chose to live alone. The Athenian jury offered Socrates the choice of a drink of hemlock or ostracism from the city-state. Socrates chose death to banishment, as the latter was a mode of life which in the opinion of the ancient Greeks was other than human. Aristotle, holding that man is essentially social, maintained that anyone who lived outside society was either an animal or a god.

The heretic chooses to think—and sometimes to act—differently from the accepted modes of his community. The heretic is unorthodox. He holds a view which is not the "correct" view. Orthodoxy is right belief measured not by a standard of absolute truth but by the number of supporters it has. An orthodoxy is right because it is held by the majority. A heresy is always the opinion of a minority. It can be the opinion of but one. The hallmark of heresy is individualism. The *Hastings Encyclopedia of Religion and Ethics* makes this point in an interesting fashion: "From the Catholic point of view Protestantism is identical with heresy. And correctly so, for Protestantism starts with the prerogative of the individual. This is the root of all heresy."[1] However, it should be added that Protestant churches easily fall into the organizational trap of forcing orthodoxy on minorities within their membership.

A heresy is wrong belief, but heresy must be carefully distinguished from heterodoxy. Heterodoxy means another belief rather than a false belief. In the language of logic the relation between orthodoxy and heterodoxy is contrariety. A heterodox belief is one that is different from another belief but not destructive of it. Contraries do not destroy each other. For example, baby blue and navy blue are contrary shades of blue. They are blendable colors. A heretical belief is one which in the minds of the orthodox is disruptive and destructive of the community of faith. To take another example, a heresy and an orthodoxy are like light and dark rather than like baby blue and navy blue. Light and dark destroy each other. When Margaret Sullivan comforted her incarcerated suffragettes, "Trust in God. She will protect you," churchmen were amused by this unusual view of the nature of God, but they were able to assimilate the new conception. However, when in recent years theologians have begun speaking of an impersonal God, a sexless God, an absentee God, and the death of God, the cry of heresy has been raised. These conceptions churchmen could not assimilate. The distinction between allowable heterodoxies and unallowable heresies may be difficult to

57

make, but it is a necessary distinction in the eyes of Christendom.

Heresy is also to be distinguished from schism and apostasy. A schismatic separates himself from the body of the church. His reasons may be doctrinal, political, moral, economic, psychological, etc. His reasons may indeed be rationalizations for his desire to be no longer identified with the church. In other words, the schismatic is anticommunal; the apostate is antidoctrinal. While there are many kinds of heretics, and while each one probably has a variety of reasons for his heresy, it is advisable to separate heresy from schism and apostasy. Many of the heretics did not wish to cut themselves off from the church. They wished to be loners in thought but not in life. They sought to reform the church, to preserve the church, to call the church back to its original and true conditions, or to urge it on to its appointed destiny, but seldom have heretics like schismatics wished to break from the church. Yet the church has usually taken stronger measures against heretics than against schismatics and apostates. The reason is obvious: schismatics and apostates openly and frankly cut themselves off respectively from the community and the faith, whereas a heretic attempts to work from within the church—until the church throws him out. Many of the heretics within Christianity wished to stay within the church. When they appeared to be desirous of destroying the church, it was the church of their day they had in mind, not the Christian Church itself. *Orthodoxy, heterodoxy,* and *heresy* always refer to beliefs at a certain time, at a certain place, and under certain conditions. Jesus was a heretic in the minds of the Jews of his day. Dostoevski in his great novel *The Brothers Karamazov* has the Grand Inquisitor say to the risen Christ from the perspective of the Russian Orthodox Church, "Tomorrow I shall condemn Thee and burn Thee at the stake as the worst of heretics." It may be a bit too facile to describe heresy as truth ill-timed. Yet today's heresies may be tomorrow's orthodoxies.

Why should the Christian Church be concerned about heresy and heretics? Is theology important? Why not let each Christian believe as he or she chooses? These are not merely academic questions to be argued only in seminaries and theological journals. Dietrich Bonhoeffer was appalled in the 1930s by what he called "cheap grace." He wrote, "Cheap grace is the daily enemy of our Church.

We are fighting today for costly grace. Cheap grace means grace sold on the market like cheapjack's wares. The sacraments, the forgiveness of sin, and the consolations of religion are thrown away at cut prices. Grace is represented as the inexhaustible treasury of the Church, from which she showers blessings with generous hands, without asking questions or fixing limits. Grace without price, grace without cost!"[2] Cheap grace is still an issue in Christianity, but were Bonhoeffer with us today, he surely would call attention to what may be named "easy belief." If cheap grace is a travesty of the Christian doctrine of the atonement, easy belief is a travesty of Christian doctrine in its entirety. "Only believe and you are saved" places very limited demands on the intellect. Easy belief may be an unplanned and undesirable by-product of the recent emphasis on the need for church involvement in social, political, and economic dimensions of modern life. The experience of the United Presbyterian Church in the United States of America is illustrative. In 1958 the General Assembly appointed a committee named "A Special Committee on a Brief Contemporary Statement of Faith." Since 1729 the Westminster Confession of Faith with two catechisms had been the confessional statement of the faith of this denomination, although amendments and additions had been made through the years. After nine years of thought and argument the Presbyterians decided to change their posture regarding the belief of their church. The denomination now holds that "confessions and declarations are subordinate standards in the church," and it sets forth as its belief a collection of creedal statements which includes the Nicene Creed, the Apostles' Creed, the Scots Confession, the Heidelberg Catechism, the Second Helvetic Confession, the Westminster Confession of Faith, the Shorter Catechism, and the Theological Declaration of Barmen. To this list is added with equal standing what is known as The Confession of 1967. The defense offered is part of the Confession of 1967: "In every age the church has expressed its witness in words and deeds as the need of the time required. . . . No one type of confession is exclusively valid, no one statement is irreformable. . . . The purpose of the Confession of 1967 is to call the church to that unity in confession and mission which is required of disciples today." The key idea in the Confession of 1967 is reconciliation; hence the three parts of the Confession are entitled "God's Work of Reconciliation," "The Ministry of Reconciliation," and "The Fulfillment of Reconciliation."

A new position has been taken by the Presbyterians on the nature and function of a creed. A confessional statement is no longer an expression of the faith finally and completely formulated, but a changing approximation of what the majority of church members believe at a particular time and place. The Confession of 1967 says of itself, "This Confession is not a 'system of doctrine,' nor does it include all the traditional topics of theology. For example, the Trinity and the Person of Christ are not redefined but are recognized and reaffirmed as forming the basis and determining the structure of the Christian faith." The Confession does contain statements on birth control and civil rights, but none on the ordination of women, abortion, or homosexuality. Ten years after its formulation this Confession needed to be updated. There is tension in this denomination because many feel that the new posture with respect to historical creeds demeans the role of Christian doctrine in favor of involvement in social and political action.

If the Presbyterian Confession of 1967 officially underplays theology, there are other evidences in Christianity which point to its resurgence. Movements such as process theology, secular theology, the Death of God theology, the theology of hope, and liberation theology are examples of its vitality. Martin E. Marty and Dean G. Peerman of *The Christian Century* edited for a number of years after 1964 a paperback of the outstanding theological articles published in the previous twelve months. They had no difficulties in finding stimulating and innovative articles. Societies have been formed in recent years designed to perpetuate the study of some of the theological giants of the twentieth century, for example, the Tillich Working Group, the Karl Barth Society, and the Bonhoeffer Society.

How did Christianity become involved in heresy hunting? Not all religions are engaged in such activities. Heresy is practically unknown in Hinduism and Buddhism, although it is found in Judaism and Islam. The factor which makes the difference is the presence or absence of a strong organization. Organizations, the membership of which is determined by commonality of belief, must insure that their members accept the essential core of doctrine. It was Christianity's struggle for survival in the Roman Empire which forced the Christian Church to develop a body of belief required of all members. Only a closely knit body of believers could survive those trying days of persecution. Another factor was the need of the Church to determine its relation to the Jewish community. And a third element was the struggle against paganism, especially against Greek philosophy.

The technique the Church used from earliest times was to require the neophyte to repeat a simple statement of belief. This formal statement was made at the time of the rite of baptism. In the New Testament can be found these minimal creeds which New Testament scholars call "rules of faith." For example, Acts 8:37 recounts the story of an Ethiopian eunuch who came to Philip asking to join the cult. Philip asked him if he believed with all his heart, and the eunuch replied, "I believe that Jesus Christ is the Son of God." On the basis of this confession of faith Philip baptized him. A verbal statement of belief in the divinity of Jesus was from the earliest times a requirement for identification with the Christian Church: "If you confess with your lips that Jesus is Lord and believe in your heart that God raised him from the dead, you will be saved."[3] Paul longed that "every tongue confess that Jesus Christ is Lord."[4] These one-line Christologies found throughout the letters of Paul are evidences of the earliest of the creeds of the Church. These creedal statements were used in four different ways: (1) as part of the baptismal ritual, (2) as a means of religious instruction, (3) as a sign for the recognition of fellow Christians, and (4) as a method for identifying heretics.

In the baptismal service the baptizand was asked, "Do you believe Jesus is the Lord?" and the reply was, "I do believe that Jesus is the Lord." When the doctrine of the Trinity was firmly established, there were three questions, three answers, and three immersions. There were many variations of the baptismal rite. One of the most interesting was the fourth century ritual of some churches in which candidates first faced west, the direction of darkness, to renounce the devil, his works, his power, and his worship; and then faced east, the direction of light, to profess belief in the Father, the Son, the Holy Spirit, and the efficacy of baptism.

By the fourth century the creeds were clearly used as part of the training for church membership. Christianity from the first was a religion of belief as well as of feeling. There was need for a simple

61

instrument for informing the inquirer what was expected in the area of belief. To strengthen the place of the creeds in the life of the Church the creeds were often repeated as part of the worship service. This was known as *traditio* (handing-out) and *redditio* (giving back). Interesting arguments are found as to the propriety of putting the creeds into writing. Some felt that the creeds should be preserved orally.

The third function of creeds is indicated in the early references to a creed as *symbolum* (sign, symbol, token). When Christianity moved into the Greek world, the Christians discovered that certain of the mystery cults, such as Eleusinia, used secret signs or passwords. "Jesus is Lord" began to be so used by the Christians. Later in Rome the sign of the fish had a similar function. The Lords Prayer was also used as a *symbolum*.

The fourth usage was to ferret out heretics. During the first three centuries the creedal statements were used largely for the instruction of laymen, but after the third century an added use was to test the orthodoxy of the clergy. In the Council of Arles (314) the bishops agreed that those suspected of heresy should be "asked the creed." It is interesting to note that inasmuch as each church by this time had its own creed, each church was in effect regarding every other church as heretical.

The earliest of the formal creeds of the Christian Church is the one known as the Old Roman Creed. It was developed in Rome within the second half of the second century. Its three-articled formula— Father, Son, and "a string of miscellaneous credentia"[5] became the pattern for other creeds. Scholars give particular attention to this creed because as J. N. D. Kelly says it was "nothing more or less than a compendium of popular theology, all the more fascinating to us because we can discern, crystallized in its clauses, the faith and hope of the primitive Church."[6] Kelly adds, "As a compendium of popular theology it might seem curiously defective, and modern people with their special interests have sometimes wondered why it contains no reference (to select three points at random) to the teaching of Jesus or to the Atonement or to the Holy Eucharist. It should be remembered, however, that creeds, as they emerged historically, were never intended to be complete summaries of the Christian faith in all its aspects."[7] All creeds developed by the Western Church may be regarded as descendents of the Old Roman Creed. The creeds of the Eastern Church also show its influence. A striking difference in the Eastern creeds is the use of *one*: "one God," "one Lord Jesus Christ," "one Holy Spirit." The earliest reliable formulation of the Old Roman Creed comes to us from the writings of Tyrannius Rufinus dated 404: "I believe in God the Father Almighty; and in Christ Jesus His Only Son, our Lord, who was born from the Holy Spirit and the Virgin Mary, who under Pontius Pilate was crucified and buried, on the third day rose again from the dead, ascended to heaven, sits at the right hand of the Father, whence He will come to judge the living and the dead; and in the Holy Spirit, the holy Church, the remission of sins, the resurrection of the flesh."

As creeds came to be used increasingly to distinguish the orthodox and the heretics, a new feature entered. This was the introduction of anathemas. The anathemas remind us that the creeds of Christendom were often the result of hot controversies among the churches. An anathema cast the offender from the church and placed a curse upon him. A creed formed by Lucian of Antioch contains a typical anathema: "Holding then this faith, and holding it from the beginning to the end, in the sight of God and of Christ we anathematize every heretical heterodoxy. And if anyone teaches contrary to the sound and right faith of the Scriptures, that time or season or age either is or has been before the generation of the Son, let him be anathema. Or if anyone say that the Son is a creature as one of the creatures, or an offspring as one of the offsprings, or a work as one of the works, and not as the divine Scriptures have handed down each of the aforesaid articles, or if he teaches or preaches besides what we have received, let him be anathema."

The Council of Ephesus (431) approved a creed containing twelve anathemas. Anathemas strike the modern Christian as being peculiarly and decidedly unChristian in spirit, but what is often forgotten is that the first five hundred years of the life of the Church was a struggle among churches and bishops. Bishops were continually coming together in councils to argue with one another over specific items of doctrine. So many bishops were rushing from one council to another between 325 and 381 that their movements were said to have disrupted the transportation system of the Roman Empire. When a modern Christian asks, "Why can't we go back to the early days of the Church when all were united in a common cause?" he reveals ignorance of the life of the early Church. As J. W. C. Wand has stated, "It is quite unrealistic to look back to some halcyon days when all Christians thought alike. There never were such days. . . . Normally the first Christian teachers agreed to differ or reached a new synthesis without serious conflict. At other times disputes came out into the open. James thought it necessary to correct the Pauline teaching about faith and works. Paul himself had a grim struggle with those who would have kept Christianity as an enclave within Judaism. John has to request that hospitality shall not be granted to false teachers."[8]

The anathemas of the early creeds call attention to an important feature of all creeds: a creed is by its nature a statement of both what ought to be believed and what ought not to be believed. A creed is a fence which both encloses and excludes. A creed identifies covertly, if not overtly, what the off-limit beliefs are. The anathemas were efforts to state what was not to be believed. But even when no anathemas were included, the notion of unallowable beliefs was adumbrated.

John Knox in an interesting book entitled *Limits of Unbelief* argues that a creed is liberal in what it encloses and specific in what it excludes. He means by this that a creed states exactly what cannot be believed by the Christian. Although the statement may be positive, the implication is negative; that is, "I believe X" actually means "I am not to believe non-X." Creeds, therefore, argues Knox, ought not to be interpreted as enforcing a narrow belief but as identifying an area within which a variety of beliefs is possible. A creed ought to be liberal in what it allows and specific in what it will not allow. A creed ought not to tell us what to believe but rather what the limits are within which we can believe as we choose. Knox writes, "Orthodoxy in our time permits many beliefs about God and says finally we cannot know or say fully and definitely what God is; heresy either says in some simple or unitary way what he is or, even more simply, denies that he is at all. Orthodoxy permits many beliefs about how it was that in Christ, God acted for us men and for our salvation and knows that no possible explanation of Christ will be adequate. Heresy either denies forthwith that such a divine action did, or could, take place or makes the same denial in less direct ways by describing the Church in purely sociological terms and by seeing it as fully contained and explained within what are understood to be the natural continuities of history. Orthodoxy is full of the hope of the life everlasting, but is unable to express the content of it in any definite way; heresy simply denies that there is such a thing."[9] Knox quotes from J. V. L. Casserley, "Heresy is much less tolerant than orthodoxy. . . . The heretic is the man who knows the precise truth. . . . The orthodox formulas, on the other hand, since they are primarily ways of negating heresy are much less specific as to what truth is."[10] Unfortunately, the Christian Church has not always been wise in creed-making. Sometimes it has tried to make its orthodox beliefs specific and rigid. Thus it has missed the wisdom Knox cherishes for the Church. Knox admits, "Orthodoxy has often been in the position of setting against the simple rigid beliefs of the heretic an equally simple and rigid belief of its own."[11]

An example of Knox's thesis is the common reference (in creeds) to God as Father. In the early Church there were at least seven orthodox interpretations of what calling God "The Father" meant. (1) God is Father only to the person renewed and reborn through divine grace. (Cyprian) (2) God is Father to the Christian in the sense that God has a closer relation to the Christian than to any other person. (Tertullian) (3) God is Father in that he is loving, compassionate, and forgiving. (Clement) (4) God is Father in his special relation to Jesus Christ. (Ignatius, Rufinus) (5) God is Father in his creative role with respect to man and the entire universe. (Clement) (6) God is Father in that he was before the universe came into being. (Theophilus) (7) God is Father in the sense of being the perfect founder of all things. (Novatian)

Part of the problem in the interpretation of creeds lies in the language of the creeds. It is often misunderstood. The language of Christian faith—and hence the language of creeds—is more like the language of art than like the language of science. It expresses what we value more than what we see, hear, taste, touch, and feel. It includes what we hope as well as what we experience. It deals with qualities and does not confine itself to what can be quantified, numbered, measured, and empirically demonstrated. The words following "I believe . . ." are not to be understood as forming statements which are factually accurate. "I believe in God the Father Almighty" is more like "I believe in the goodness of mankind" than like "I believe High Street is north of Graham Street" or "I believe this sum is correct." The language of belief is richly metaphorical. For example, Christian creeds ought to contain a footnote like this: "We do not mean that God is actually a father, i.e., one who sired a child upon a woman. We do not actually believe that God is male, but we do want to insist that our relationship to God is personal in some form. We refer to God as King and Shepherd, but we do not mean that God reigns as a monarch nor that God herds sheep."

The heretics and the church form a far more vital union than either is willing to admit. The idea that Christianity was unified at the beginning will not stand the test of casual examination, as we have already noted. Christians have desired unity, but unity remains a hope, not a reality. A new evaluation of heretics is in order. The heretics share with the saints religious vitality. Heretics cared enough about Christian thought to put their lives on the line. Many heretics were also martyrs—but not for orthodoxy. As Walter Nigg has said, "The view that heretics were wicked men whose fate need not concern the Christian has been widely propagated. For centuries heretics were defamed in every possible way. The aim has always been to spread a forbidding and repulsive picture of heretics."[12] This evaluation must be completely overthrown in favor of the view of Augustine, one of the greatest heresy hunters of all time. Augustine in his essay "Of True Religion," 1. 15, takes a text from I Corinthians 11:19, "For there must be also heresies among you, that they which are approved may be made manifest among you," to argue that the light of heretics can lead to God's light: "Let us make use of that gift of divine providence. Men become heretics who would have no less held wrong opinions even within the Church. Now that they are outside they do us more good, not by teaching the truth, for they do not know it, but by provoking carnal Catholics to seek the truth and spiritual Catholics to expound it. There are in the Holy Church innumerable men approved by God, but they do not become manifest among us so long as we are delighted with the darkness of ignorance, and prefer to sleep rather than to behold the light of truth. So, many are awakened from sleep by the heretics, so they may see God's light and be glad."[13]

NOTES

1. Vol. 6, p. 614.
2. Dietrich Bonhoeffer, *The Cost of Discipleship.* Trans. by R. H. Fuller. (New York: The Macmillan Co., 1949), p. 37.
3. Romans 10:9. The Revised Standard Version is used throughout this study.
4. Philippians 2:11.
5. *Early Christian Creeds.* (New York: David McKay Co., 1972), p. 152.
6. *Ibid.*, p. 131.
7. *Ibid.*, p. 165.
8. J. W. C. Wand, *The Four Great Heresies.* (London: A. R. Mowbray and Co., 1955), p. 20.
9. John Knox, *Limits of Unbelief.* (London: Collins, 1970), p. 25.
10. *Ibid.*
11. *Ibid.*, p. 26.
12. Walter Nigg, *The Heretics.* Trans. by Richard and Clara Winston. (New York: Alfred A. Knopf, 1962), p. 5.
13. *Library of Christian Classics*, vol. 6, (Philadelphia: The Westminster Press, 1950), p. 233.

6. On Taking Myths Seriously

Although almost everyone who studies myths advises that myths be taken seriously, I wish to argue that the admonition is ambiguous until one knows what the advisor means by the term *myth*. "Myths should be taken seriously" is an incomplete sentence. "Myths should be taken seriously as . . . what?"

According to Aristotle "into the subleties of the mythically inclined it is not worth our while to inquire seriously."[1] He used "his titanic scientific intellect without recourse to Platonic myths."[2] Yet there are one hundred and thirty-two references to passages from the *Iliad* and the *Odyssey* in the extant works of Aristotle.[3] Aristotle offered as one reason for his evaluation the use of myths as a device to manipulate the common people: "our ancestors in past ages have handed down to their posterity myths . . . for the persuasion of the multitude and for legal and social uses."[4] Myths, he added, are not museum pieces: "These myths have been preserved to the present times like ancient relics."[5] Yet he did concede that the mythmaker is a quasi-philosopher: " . . . even the lover of myths is in a sense a lover of wisdom, for the myth is composed of wonders."[6] Aristotle was not averse to using myths when they suited his purposes, e.g., *On the Motion of Animals* 669 b 32 and *Generation of Animals* 716 a 13, nor to repeating a myth as fact, e.g., that Italus, King of Oenotria, lent his name to Italy.[7] Aristotle, shortly before his death, wrote a letter which seems to indicate a change of evaluation: "The more solitary and isolated I am, the more I have come to love myths."[8] Bernard J. F. Lonergan comments as follows on this letter: "Aristotle in a late letter confessed that as he grew older he became less a philosopher, a friend of wisdom, and more a friend of myths."[9] Lonergan makes far too much of this reputed letter of Aristotle. Aristotle did not state nor imply that he had become "less a philosopher." The letter was written at Chalcis in Euboea where he lived in a house owned by his

68

mother's family. When the death of Alexander had been confirmed, the latent anti-Macedonian feeling of the Athenians surfaced. Aristotle fled the city lest the Athenians "sin twice against philosophy." The sudden shift from a busy life as master of the Lyceum to a solitary life at Chalcis, plus his deteriorating health, must have turned his active mind to contemplation on the brevity of human existence. This was the situation in which he came "to love myths." But becoming "a friend of myths" did not necessarily mean he had ceased to be "a friend of wisdom." In addition, we should note that Aristotle said he had become a lover of *myths*, not a lover of *mythmakers* or *mythologists*. There is no evidence that Aristotle changed his opinion that the subtleties of mythcreators are not worth serious consideration.

Many modern scholars take myths seriously—anthropologists, ethnologists, historians, linguists, literary critics, philosophers of religion, psycho-analyists, psychologists, sociologists, theologians, etc. A common assumption of anthropologists is that, since myths are important in primitive cultures, myths are important in all cultures. Bronislaw Malinowski was especially prone to this universalistic interpretation of myths. He observed that myth "in its primitive form, is not merely a story told but a reality lived . . . not an idle tale, but a hard-working force . . . [which] expresses, enhances, and codifies belief, . . . safeguards and enforces morality, . . . vouches for the efficiency of ritual and contains practical rules for the guidance of man."[10] He concluded, "Myth is, therefore, an indispensable ingredient of all culture."[11] Although Malinowski had written on the previous page, "I have dealt in this book with savage myths, and not with the myths of culture," he never hesitated to generalize from primitive culture to all cultures. G. S. Kirk critizes Malinowski's universalism, but he agrees about the seriousness of myths. Kirk says that "myths tend to possess that element of 'seriousness' in establishing and confirming rights and institutions or exploring and reflecting problems or pre-occupations."[12] He thinks folktales differ from myths in that "they are not primarily concerned with 'serious' subjects."[13] Myths "often have some serious underlying purpose beyond that of telling a story."[14] Karl Jaspers also universalized mythmaking: "Mythical thinking is not a thing of the past, but characterizes man in any epoch."[15]

The philosopher Wilbur M. Urban warned, "Of the myth we may say: because it is not to be taken literally it does not follow that it is not to be taken seriously."[16] Alan M. Olson stated that the collection of essays he edited is "the well-reasoned views of scholars from various disciplines who ask that we take myth and symbol seriously."[17] H. and H. A. Frankfort offered a reason for taking myths seriously: "Myth, then, is to be taken seriously, because it reveals a significant, if unverifiable, truth—we might say a metaphysical truth."[18] Joseph Campbell is almost alarmist in his argument for taking myths seriously in a literal fashion, "by anyone with even a kindergarten education," he continues, "and in this there is serious danger . . . since life . . . requires life-supporting illusions; and where these have been dispelled, there is nothing secure to hold on to, no moral law, nothing firm."[19] Campbell adds that "it has always been on myths that the moral orders of society have been founded."[20]

David Bidney—philosopher and anthropologist—gave a different reason for taking myths seriously. Myth he said, must "be taken seriously precisely in order that it may be gradually superseded in the interests of the advancement of truth and the growth of human intelligence."[21] According to Susanne K. Langer, myth "is taken with religious seriousness, either as historical fact or as a 'mystic truth.'"[22] She adds that myth has "a far more difficult and serious purpose than fairytale."[23] Emil Brunner was so impressed by the serious aspect of myths that he referred to the "absolute seriousness" of the content of the Christian myth and to the manner in which the content is taken as "absolutely seriously," and concluded with a peculiar obsrvation: "In the full sense of the word we can only be 'serious' when we believe in the truth of the Christian 'myth.'"[24] Franz Boas wrote, "It would not be fair to assume that the myths dealing with the origins of the world or of the gifts of art and ceremonials to mankind were the result of a light play of imagination, as we suppose the rather insignificant tales to have been. The importance of the subject matter and the seriousness with which they are treated suggest that they were the result of thought about the origin of the world and of wonder about cultural achievements and the meaning of sacred rites."[25] Alan W. Watts noted that mythology "has only quite recently become a subject of serious study."[26]

A few students of myth qualify the note of seriousness. For example, Joseph Campbell says that mythic themes are sometimes "taken lightly . . . in a spirit of play" as "tales told for amusement," but he adds immediately that "they appear also in religious contexts, where they are accepted not only as factually true but even as revelations of the verities to which the whole culture is a living witness and from which it derives both its spiritual authority and its temporal power."[27] Philip Wheelwright said the tone of myths is "playful seriousness." He distinguished the "vehicle" of a myth and the "tenor" of a myth. The vehicle may be concrete, e.g., the avatars of Viṣṇu; or abstract, e.g., the language of a Christian creed. The tenor is a tension between superstitious literalism and transcendental allegorism. Wheelwright says, "The primitively mytho-religious attitude in its most characteristic forms has tended to settle into some kind of fertile tension between these two extremes without yielding too completely to either of them. So far as the mythic storyteller is half-consciously aware of the tension his narrative may achieve that tone of serious playfulness which characterizes so charmingly much early myth."[28] Johan Huizinga also found a modified seriousness: "In all the wild imaginings of mythology a fanciful spirit is playing on the border-line of jest and seriousness."[29]

The author of the information on "Myth" in *Webster's New Dictionary of Synonyms* astutely observes, "Myth varies considerably in its denotation and connotation depending on the persuasion of the user." The connotation which causes problems for the serious student is the "mythical" character of myth. The *Oxford English Dictionary* (1933 edition) offers only three definitions of *Myth*. (1) "A purely fictitious narrative usually involving supernatural persons, actions, or events, and embodying some popular idea concerning natural and historical phenomena." (2) "A fictitious or imaginary person or object." (3) "Combination like myth-creating, myth-making, myth-maker." The authors of *The Shorter Oxford Dictionary* (1978 edition) are also unaware that the word *myth* has much wider and different meanings. On the other hand, the editors of the seventh edition of *The Concise Oxford Dictionary of Current English* (1982), having discovered the new meaning of *myth*, offer the following definition: "Traditional narrative, usually involving supernatural or fancied persons, etc. and embodying popular ideas on natural or social phenomena, etc.; such narratives collectively; allegory (Platonic

71

myth); fictitious person or thing or idea." It is interesting to note that fictitiousness no longer has top billing! But the connotation of fictitiousness lingers. An interesting example is a book entitled *Man Against Myth*.[30] The author, Barrows Dunham, does not offer a definition of myth, but what he means by the term is indicated from scattered comments in the book, viz., a belief not in accord with facts,[31] which may contain a core of truth or an atmosphere of truth,[32] which assumes or implies absurdities,[33] which is overlaid with ambiguity,[34] and which paralyzes action toward a better world or stimulates action toward a worse one.[35] Occasionally he uses what he regards as synonyms of *myth*, e.g., *tradition,[36] prejudice,[37] mysticism,[38] superstition,[39]* and *double talk.[40]* The "myths" Dunham examines are these: "You can't change human nature," "The rich are fit and the poor unfit," "There are superior and inferior races," "There are two sides to every question," "Thinking makes it so," "You can't mix art and politics," "You have to look after yourself," "All problems are merely verbal," "Words will never hurt me," and "You cannot be free and safe." Perhaps the term *cliché* would be more appropriate than the term *myth*. I find it strange that David Bidney praises Dunham's book.[41] Yet Bidney advises, "We must distinguish . . . between myth and superstition."[42] Bidney singles out as an example of such confusion *A Treasury of American Superstitions* (1948), written by Claudia DeLys. But I think Dunham's own book is an example of the same confusion.

As a method of estimating the extent to which the term *myth* has the designation of being mythical, fictitious, false, illusory, mistaken, and non-existent, I recently examined *Books in Print 1983-1984* (New York and London: Bowker, 1983) and *British Books in Print 1983* (London: Whittaker, 1983) and discovered sixty books listed the titles of which begin *Myth of . . .* The remaining words of the titles are as follows: *Africa; the All; the All-Destructive Fury of the Thirty Years' War; Analysis; Appalachian Brain Drain; the Birth of a Hero; Black Capitalism; Blood; Britannica; Captain Cook; Christian Beginnings; the Cross; the Deprived Child; Educational Reform; the Eternal Return; Evolution; the Farm Family; Freedom; the French Revolution; God Incarnate; the Golden Years; the Great Depression; the Great Secret; the Greener Grass; a Guilty Nation; Hiawatha; Home Ownership; the Hyperactive Child; the Lazy Native; Leadership; Liberation; the Machine; the Magus; Marginality; the*

Mind; Masculinity; Mass Culture; of Mau Mau; Meaning; Mental Illness; Metaphor; Modernity; the Monstrous Male; Mormon Inspiration; Motherhood; the Negro Past; Over-Population; Petrol Power; Psychotherapy; Rome's Fall; the Ruling Class; Science; Senility; Sisyphus; Social Cost; Soviet Military Supremacy; Tantalus; the Twentieth Century; the Universal Church; Victory. Even without reading these books, one is aware that most of the authors use the term *myth* as synonymous with "false conception," "wrong idea," "misleading notion," "incorrect judgment," "erroneous opinion," "mistaken conviction," "commonly held but wrong view," "deceptively held belief," and "illusion."

The English word *myth* comes from the Greek *muthos*. According to Liddell's and Scott's dictionary the first meaning of *muthos*—first in time—is "word" (especially, mere word), "speech," "fact," "thing said," "command," "charge," "saying"; and the second meaning—second in time—is "tale," "fable," "story," "legend," "narrative," "likely story," "plot," "fiction." These two meanings adumbrate a significant change in the culture of ancient Greece. Prior to the fourth century B.C. *muthos* referred to the stories of the Olympian gods. At that time *muthos* meant "This is the word—and you better believe it!" A myth was a decisive, final pronouncement. Myth was history—or to state this conversely, history was a recorded myth. *Muthos* carried the connotation of command, charge, statement of mission, an *ipso facto*. There was even the connotation of threat to anyone who did not accept it as final: "take it—or leave it!" But by the fourth century B.C. the dramatists and philosophers of the Greek "Enlightenment" had brought about a great change: a change from how life *looks* to what life *means*, from ideas *en sita* to ideas in the mind. *Muthos* became *logos*. *Logos* also means "word"—but a different sort of word. *Logos* means reckoning, explanation, reason, ground, formula. A mythical statement prior to the fourth century B.C. was a command: "Look! See! Believe!" A myth was not only about the gods, but also a statement that carried its own Olympic sanction. A myth was a telling of the way things are. There was no connotation of unreality. Acquiescence was the proper response. But during the sixth, fifth, and fourth centuries B.C. the myths of the gods became likely stories—and, finally, misleading stories, even plots designed to deceive.

Pindar was one of the first of the Greeks to associate *muthos* with falsehood. Herodotus rejected as mythical the tradition that the River Ocean encircled the world. Euhemerus of Messene rationalized the Olympian gods as heroes falsely raised to divine status.

The word *myth* has never regained its former status. As Mircea Eliade has observed, "If in every European language the word 'myth' denotes a 'fiction,' it is because the Greeks proclaimed it to be such twenty-five centuries ago."[43] This seems also to be the historical root of the "broken myth"—a myth known to be a myth, i.e., a falsehood—which Paul Tillich identifies and deplores. Bidney conjectures that Christianity is largely responsible for having reduced the Greek and Roman myths to "discarded and incredible narratives."[44] This, however, ignores some interesting facts about Christianity and Christians. Justin Martyr, the first Christian to die for the faith, in his *Apology* (c. 150) wrote that "those who live according to reason are Christians, even though they are accounted atheists. Such were Socrates and Heraclitus among the Greeks."[45] Also Clement of Alexandria in *Stromateis* (c. 200) claimed, "Philosophy was a 'schoolmaster' to bring the Greek mind to Christ, as the Law brought the Hebrews. Thus philosophy was a preparation, paving the way towards the perfection in Christ."[46] Bidney also forgets that the Greeks had begun a celebration-lamentation of the death of their gods five hundred years before Christianity appeared on the scene. Account should also be taken of the restoration of the Greek gods into the heavenly pantheon in the Renaissance-Reformation. For example, Zwingli wrote a letter to Francis I in which he advised, "Shouldst thou follow in the footsteps of David, thou wilt one day see God Himself; and near to Him thou mayest hope to see Adam, Abel, Enoch, Paul, Hercules, Theseus, Socrates. . ."[47]

Logos picked up where *muthos* left off. The *logos* about the gods became a claim to truth, not a declaration of truth. A *logos* truth is one that can be argued for, demonstrated, and supported by evidence. When the author of the Fourth Gospel wrote his witness, he stated, "In the beginning was the Logos . . ." rather than "In the beginning was the Mythos. . ." We may assume that he meant that his Gospel was not one which presented Christianity as the fulfillment of the *Torah* as did Matthew, nor as a straightforward presentation of facts as did Mark, nor as a historical record as did Luke, but as a treatise supported by rational evidence.

Meanwhile the Olympians had been demythologized, i.e., they had been demoted from their earlier ontic status in at least three ways. One was the way of rationalization; e.g., Thales stated the gods are not on Mt. Olympus or in any transcendental realm. According to him the gods are in things. The gods as loci of growth, change, development, and alteration are found within natural objects. A second way of demotion was allegorization. Thagenes said the names of the gods in the Homeric epics represent either human faculties or natural elements. A third method was euhemerism, i.e., the claim that the gods are ancient kings deified. Myths, according to euhemerism, are the records of the apotheosis of human beings.

Myth was introduced into Christian theology early in the nineteenth century as a hermeneutical device especially in respect to the Gospel accounts of Jesus the Christ. D. G. Strauss in his *Life of Jesus* (1835) distinguished three kinds of myths: (1) historical myths, i.e., narratives of actual events colored by thought forms of the time; (2) philosophical myths, i.e., ideas clothed in narrative form; (3) poetical myths, i.e., historical or philosophical myths veiled in poetic fancy. When he wrote his *Life of Jesus* he thought the myth-making process was not planned, but in his *New Life of Jesus* (1865) he admitted that he had changed his mind and accepted the notion of "conscious and intentional mythologizing."

Definitions are will-o'-the-wisps. Even when a scholar knows that the object or act or idea defies definition, he cannot resist the effort to define—although he often prefaces the definition with a warning to the reader that the "definition" is not really a definition. G. S. Kirk, for example, cautions about definitions of myth: "There is no one definition of myth, no Platonic form of a myth against which all actual instances can be measured. Myths . . . differ enormously in their morphology and their social function."[48] Maurice Wills warns, "Insistence on a very precise definition of myth usually turns out to be part of a Pyrrhic victory in which the author succeeds in proving the points he wants to make about myth by the simple process of making them true by definition."[49] Some of the "definitions" of myth and mythology are merely short descriptions with chiefly mnemonic value, e.g., "a verbal misapprehension or disease of language,"[50] "the science of a pre-scientific age,"[51] "psychology misread as biography, history, and cosmology,"[52] "the depersonalized dream,"[53] "history turned into fable,"[54] "an ambush of reality,"[55] "a natural prologue to philosophy,"[56] "a definite form of the cultural interpretation of existence,"[57] "the symbolization of the infinite,"[58] "the idea of a credible impossibility,"[59] and "a numinous story."[60]

Many students of mythology have tried seriously to formulate a definition of myth. I offer the following as some of the better examples:

1. ". . . every unhistorical narrative—however it may have originated—in which a religious community recognizes a constituent part of its sacred origins as an absolute expression of its fundamental sentiments and ideas."[61]
2. " . . . a doctrine expressed in a narrative form, an abstract moral or spiritual truth dramatized in action and personification; where the object is to enforce faith not in the parable but in the moral."[62]
3. "Myth narrates a sacred history; it relates an event that took place in primordial time, the fables time of the 'beginning.' . . . [Myth] is always an account of a 'creation'; it relates how something was produced, began to be."[63]
4. ". . . essentially a story. Its characters may be divinities or demons, heroes or slaves; its plots may be beautiful or terrifying; but these are conceived of imaginatively, and fantasy may serve their truths. Mythmaking is an artistic endeavor to capture a common experience or understanding, or idea, or activity in pictographs and symbols; its form is nonliterate and often irrational."[64]
5. ". . . belief usually expressed in narrative form that is incompatible with scientific knowledge."[65]
6. ". . . thoughts, feelings, and actions that are inconsistent with the findings of natural science."[66]
7. ". . . a story, the spontaneous product of unreflective and uncritical consciousness in which the forces of nature are represented in personal or quasi-personal forms and as performing supernatural and superpersonal functions."[67]
8. ". . . a story which is told but which is not literally true, or an idea or image which is applied to someone or something but which does not literally apply but which invites a particular attitude in its hearers."[68]

9. ". . . a story rooted in a place where one has been in the past and that one has to reach urgently in the present and that someone at a crucial point on the way says did not exist."[69]

10. ". . . a type of narrative which seeks to express in imaginative form a belief about man, the world or deity which cannot be expressed in simple propositions."[70]

11. ". . . a tale to be conveyed and to be verified by nothing else than the act of telling it. A myth that can be proved or verified by something outside of the living oral or written religious tradition is not really myth. Thus the only good definition of myth is that myth neither requires nor includes any possible verification of itself."[71]

12. ". . . the use of imagery to express the otherworldly in terms of this world and the divine in terms of human life, the other side in terms of this side."[72]

13. ". . .the error of mythologizing reality, of taking language literally instead of metaphorically."[73]

14. ". . . a complex of stories—some no doubt fact, and some fantasy— which, for various reasons, human beings regard as demonstrations of the inner meaning of the universe and of human life."[74]

15. ". . . a complex of images or a story, whether factual or fanciful, taken to represent the deepest truths of life, or simply regarded as specially significant for no clearly realized reason."[75]

16. ". . . an enactment in time of an event or principle whose reality is actually beyond history but which, except when it is clearly legendary, has meaning only in relation to human destiny."[76]

17. ". . . a story which has come down from the past, which ostensibly relates a historical event or events, and of which the origin has been lost or forgotten."[77]

18. ". . . a story which cannot with any success be reasonably accredited, but which is accepted without reasoning to such an extent that people act on its assumptions."[78]

19. ". . . a story or a complex of story elements taken as expressing, and therefore as implicitly symbolizing, certain deep-lying aspects of human and transhuman existence."[79]

20. ". . . a narrative, in whatever form, that recounts the doings of gods, heroes, and humans before the dawn of history."[80]

21. ". . . the ultimate, undefinable expression of an essentially undifferentiated ('pre-philosophic') thought which, in contrast to structured, articulated or conceptual thinking, intuitively formulates and comprehends something within and through itself."[81]

If I were to distill a definition of myth from the above twenty-one definitions, I would be liable to Maurice Will's charge of proving the points I want to make by making them true by definition. Yet I think it is not unreasonable to note certain common features of these definitions. The first is that a myth is a story. The word *story* appears in nine of the definitions, the word *narrative* in six, and word *tale* in one. There seems to be no significant difference among the three terms. Gerald S. Hawkins in his fascinating book, *Stonehenge Decoded,*[82] may carry synonymity too far. In the first seven pages of this book he uses the following words interchangeably: *myth,*[83] *story,*[84] *legend,*[85] *speculation,*[86] *fable,*[87] *folk lore,*[88] *fairy tale,*[89] *tale,*[90] and *poetic theory.*[91] It is also interesting to note that in the index the item "Myth" contains only one citation—"See Legends."

Into what general class should myths be placed, assuming that myth itself is not the name of the class? The candidates are epic, fable, fairy tale, fiction, folklore, folk tale, history, legend, narrative, parable, saga, story, tale, and yarn. From this group of possible classes I select narrative. My reason for selection is well stated in *Castell's Modern Guide to Synonyms and Related Words:* "All these words refer to the verbal account of an occurrence, whether real or imaginary. Narrative is the most formal and general of these."[92] The word *story* is secondary: "Story can function as an informal substitute for narrative in many instances."[93]

What *kind* of narrative is myth? The twenty-one definitions offer some guidance, although the judgment is rather subjective. My judgment is that eight of the twenty-one stress the non-historical features of myth, viz., definitions 1, 3, 4, 6, 9, 10, 16, 17; that five stress the moral or spiritual truths of the content, viz., definitions 2, 12, 14, 19, 20; that four emphasize the unverifiability of myth, viz., definitions 5, 11, 18, 21; and that four note that a myth is fictitious viz., definitions 7, 8, 13, 15. This would suggest the following working definition of myth: a narrative of trans-historical events told to reinforce spiritual or moral teachings.

Myth as used in this essay never denotes a lie. Myth as lie is a vulgar usage which surfaces when myth is defined as fictitious narrative. To think of a myth as a false tale is to confuse literal truth and symbolic truth. Myth as a literary genre is to be classified with poetry. "I wandered lonely as a cloud" may be a true statement of one's emotional state, but it certainly does not describe how I traveled from Rome to Florence! Taking myths seriously does not mean taking them literally. The nonpoetic person would do well to eschew myths altogether.

The subclasses of myth are commonly said to be three: (1)myths proper, (2) myths of legends, and (3) folk tale myths. H. J. Rose describes the three subclasses as those which are "a kind of imaginative precursor of scientific investigation," those which "have behind them real events," and those which are "pure fiction and seem to have no other origin than a desire to amuse and interest." But he admits immediately, "In any given story of sufficient length and elaboration, elements of more than one kind of traditional tale, or of all three may be found."[94] Similar three-fold classifications appear in *Funk and Wagnalls' Standard Dictionary of Folklore, Mythology and Legend* and in *Index to Fairy Tales, Myths and Legends*.[95] Katherine M. Briggs in her book *A Dictionary of British Folk-tales*[96] divides folk tales into "folk narratives," i.e., "folk fiction, told for edification, delight or amusement"[97] and "folk legends," i.e., stories "once believed to be true."[98]

The *Standard Dictionary of Folklore, Mythology and Legend* maintains that the characters in myths are deities, whereas those in legends and folk tales are not deities; that myths are related to other stories, whereas legends and folk tales are not so related; and that legends are limited to a specific location, whereas myths and folk tales are not so limited. These—and similar comparisons and contrasts—are so subjective that I question their value. Legends, myths, and folk tales sometimes do change into each other, in spite of their differences. For example, by the fourth century B.C. the Greek myths had become folk tales. The cry "Great Pan is dead" marked the end of the reign of the Olympians and the beginning of what Gilbert Murray called "a failure of nerve." A five-year-old child today may have similar feelings of loss as the child moves from the Santa Claus myth to the discovery "Santa Claus is just my dad." Rudolf Bultmann in the early 1950s aroused great controversy in some Christian circles with his essay in which he recommended the demythologization (*Entmythologisierung*) of the New Testament. It is interesting to note that in this essay he referred to the Virgin Birth not as a myth but as a legend. Thus he not only avoided the connotation of fictitiousness but also by not using the word *myth* avoided a heresy, since the word *legend* located parthenogenesis in history.[99]

One of the ways to study myths seriously and to distinguish myths from other narrative forms is to consider the motives of the narrator. A consideration of the ten following motives is highly relevant for this aspect of the study of myths:

1. To entertain. Narrations can be fun, especially when told in the proper voice, at a proper time of day, at a particular place, and to an appreciative audience.

2. To explain. By use of narratives people can learn about the origin of the world, gods, natural phenomena, human beings, customs, rituals, sickness, and death. They can be encouraged to think about values and last things.

3. To present a view of the world—a *Weltanschauung*—that will capture the imagination of the hearers. Often they are encouraged to think of the world in personal terms.

4. To establish a sense of mystery. Through narratives men and women can experience the numinous, the holy. Fear, dread, and awe can be fostered by pictorial images offered by the narrator. The hearers are led to experience the *mysterium tremendum* of the life of which they are a part.

5. To maintain the social structure. Traditions are preserved through the retelling of past events, often in the imagined life of a culture hero. Many so-called "modern myths" are ideologies, e.g., the Führer-principle, Rosenberg's Myth of the Twentieth Century, the Proletarian Man in Marxism, and the story of the battle of Lapiths and Centaurs as recorded on the metope of the Parthenon.

6. To integrate lives of individuals. Narrations may be used to call to mind archetypal urges and future aspirations. Freud's appeal to childhood experiences and Jung's appeal to cosmic consciousness were psychoanalytic uses of myths.

7. To support what is already believed. Narratives can be used to strengthen faith, support values, validate accepted beliefs, encourage acceptance of traditions, and justify creedal statements. Thomas Kuhn in *The Structure of Scientific Revolution*[100] uses the word *paradigm* to refer to a set of assumptions—a "super-theory"—within which a science functions. Karl Mannheim used the term "ideology" for the same unexamined framework of thinking in social and political contexts.[101] *Uncle Tom's Cabin, The Adventures of Tom Sawyer,* and *The*

Adventures of Huckleberry Finn present in fictional form social assumptions analyzed by Kuhn and Mannheim.

8. To celebrate the human estate. The human being can, through narratives, experience satisfaction and pride in his position between animals and gods.

9. To comfort the sorrowing. In narratives the sufferings of the human condition can be put in perspective.

10. To challenge. The narration can be an instrument of inspiration, encouragement, and enthusiasm.

My assumption in formulating the above list of ten motivations of narration is that narrators of folk tales, legends, and myths will contend that all ten motivations are operative in their narrations and that one is primary. While it would be unrealistic to assume that each class of narrator will agree on the ranking of the ten motivations in order of priority, it is not unrealistic to note which motivaion is of greatest importance for each class of narrator.

In my opinion the narrator of folk tales qua folk tales is motivated primarily by the desire to entertain, i.e., by motive #1. Folk tales are told to amuse the hearers. If the folk tale makes a moral point, that is subordinate to entertainment. Does the tale of Jack and the Beanstalk explain anything, teach anything, encourage, or comfort? Perhaps it could under some circumstances, but the chief motive for telling the story is to amuse.

The narrator of legends qua legends is chiefly concerned about maintaining the social structure. This is motive #5. Legends are often of how things were in the "olden days." The exploits of Daniel Boone, John Bull, Uncle Sam, Abraham, Isaac, Jacob, and Pecos Bill fill the hearers with pride and establish the historical continuity of a people.

The narrator of myths qua myths is motivated by fideism, i.e., by motive #7. The mythmaker or mythteller does not seek to explain or entertain. The question the narrator answers is not the question "Why?" but the question "How—if not thus?" What he says is neither true nor false. He does not, except incidentally, challenge, encourage, celebrate, comfort, provide psychological integration, cultivate mystery, stimulate imagination, or entertain. He is an establishment person. He speaks in support of the *status quo*. If the

81

narrator of myth does anything other than support what is already believed, that is tangential to the main task. His mission is to undergird the received faith. If the narrator becomes concerned about instruction, he becomes a teacher; if more concerned about amusement, he becomes an entertainer; if more concerned about comforting, he becomes a priest.

If this is what the mythmaker and mythteller are intending, the question "Are myths necessary?" is highly relevant. Do societies need the support which only myth can give? W. M. Urban argues for what he calls the "indispensable myth," by which he means types of mythological symbolism indispensable to religion if religion is to be more than an empty abstraction, to epistemology if man is to apprehend reality directly, and to language if language is to be ultimately effective.[102] Myth, for Urban, connotes pictorialization, and there is no denying that concrete images are effective in communication. Plato, one of the most subtle of Western philosophers, was also the philosopher who made lavish use of myths. However, does Plato's use of myth justify the use of myths today? G. S. Kirk refers sarcastically to "man's endearing insistence on carrying quasi-mythical modes of thought . . . into a supposedly scientific age."[103] Alan Watts was equally sarcastic when he attacked those who hold "the notion that poetry and myth belong to the realm of fancy as distinct from fact, and since facts equal truth, myth and poetry have no serious content."[104] But little is gained by such attacks or defenses. What is needed is a serious study of myth. Far too often, as Kirk states, "myth as a general concept is completely vague."[105] According to *Funk and Wagnalls' Dictionary of Folklore, Mythology and Legend,* "No single explanation of myth yet set forth is fully satisfactory."[106] Eliade, who has done so much work on primitive religions, proclaims—perhaps too optimistically—, "We are at last beginning to know and understand the value of the myth."[107] At least we are aware we need science to learn about our world, philosophy to examine the quality of our life, and myth to conserve our traditional wisdom. We need also to study seriously our sciences, our philosophies, and our myths. Man-at-his-best is philomath, philosopher, and philomythicist.

NOTES

1. *Alla peri men tōn muthikōs sophixomenōn ouk axion meta spoudēs skopein.*
   (Metaphysics 1000 a 18.) Both W. D. Ross in the Oxford translations and
   Hugh Tredennick in the Loeb Classical Library translate *muthikōs* as
   "mythologists," but I doubt very much that Aristotle was warning
   against those who *study* myths. Surely he had in mind those who *make* or
   tell myths.
2. R. C. Zaehner, *Our Savage God.* (London: Collins, 1974), p. 191.
3. See my *An Index to Aristotle.* (Princeton: Princeton University Press,
   1949), pp. 78-79.
4. *Metaphysics* 1074 b 11.
5. *Ibid.*
6. *Ibid.,* 982 b 17.
7. *Politics* 1329 b 9-18.
8. See Werner Jaeger, *Aristotle.* Trans. by Richard Robinson. (Oxford:
   Clarendon Press, 1934), p. 321. According to Anton-Hermann Chroust,
   "Aristotle must have been a terrifyingly lonely man . . . a reserved,
   austere and solitary man, withdrawn into himself and hidden from the
   world by the unconquerable ramparts of his awesome learning." *Aristotle.* (Notre Dame, Indiana: University of Notre Dame Press, 1973), vol.
   1, p. 246.
9. "Reality, Myth, Symbol" in *Myth, Symbol and Reality,* ed. by Alan M.
   Olson. (Notre Dame and London: Notre Dame University Press, 1980),
   p. 33.
10. *Magic, Science and Religion and Other Essays.* (Garden City, N.Y.: Double-
    day, 1954), pp. 100, 101.
11. *Ibid.*
12. *Myth: Its Meaning and Functions in Ancient and Other Cultures.* (Cambridge:
    Cambridge University Press, 1970), p. 40.
13. *Ibid.,* p. 37.
14. *Ibid.,* p. 41.
15. "Myth and Religion" in *Kerygma and Myth,* ed. by H. W. Barsch, trans.
    by Reginald H. Fuller. (London: S.P.C.K., 1953), p. 144.
16. *Language and Reality.* (London: George Allen and Unwin, 1939), p. 593.
17. *Myth, Symbol and Reality,* p. 2.
18. *The Intellectual Adventure of Ancient Man.* (Chicago: University of Chicago
    Press, 1946), p. 7.
19. *Myths to Live By.* (London: Souvenir Press, 1973), p. 10.
20. *Ibid.,* p. 11.

21. "Myth, Symbolism, and Truth" in *Myth: A Symposium*, ed. by Thomas Sebeok. (Bloomington: Indiana University Press, 1958), p. 14.
22. *Philosophy in a New Key.* (Cambridge: Harvard University Press, 1957), p. 175.
23. *Ibid.*, p. 176.
24. *The Mediator*, trans. by Olive Wyon. (London: Butterworth, 1934), pp. 387, 386, 393.
25. *General Anthropology.* (New York: Heath, 1938), p. 616.
26. *Myth and Ritual in Christianity.* (London and New York: Thames and Hudson, 1953), p. 5.
27. "The Historical Development of Mythology" in *Myth and Mythmaking*, ed. by Henry A. Murray. (New York: Braziller, 1960), p. 19.
28. "The Semantic Approach to Myth" in *Myth: A Symposium*, ed. by Thomas A. Sebeok. (Bloomington: Indiana University Press, 1958), p. 103.
29. *Homo Ludens*, trans. by R. F. C. Hull. (London: Routledge and Kegan Paul, 1949), p. 5.
30. Barrows Dunham, *Man Against Myth.* (London: Frederick Muller, 1948).
31. *Ibid.*, p. 32.
32. *Ibid.*, p. 28.
33. *Ibid.*, p. 32.
34. *Ibid.*, p. 28.
35. *Ibid.*, p. 32.
36. *Ibid.*, p. 76.
37. *Ibid.*, p. 81.
38. *Ibid.*, p. 92.
39. *Ibid.*, p. 104.
40. *Ibid.*, p. 221.
41. "The Concept of Myth and the Problem of Psychocultural Evolution." *American Anthropologist*, vol. 52, (1950), p. 25.
42. *Ibid.*, p. 23.
43. *Myth and Reality.* (London: George Allen and Unwin, 1964), p. 148.
44. "Myth, Symbolism, and Truth" in *Myth: a Symposium*, p. 1.
45. *Documents of the Christian Church.* 2d ed. Selected and ed. by Henry Bettenson. (London: Oxford University Press, 1963), p. 6.
46. *Ibid.*, p. 9.
47. Jean Seznec, *The Survival of the Pagan Gods: The Mythological Tradition and Its Place in Renaissance Humanism and Art.* (New York: Pantheon Books, 1953), p. 23.
48. *Myth: Its Meaning and Functions in Ancient and Other Cultures*, p. 7.

49. "Myth in Theology" in *The Myth of God Incarnate*, ed. by John Hick. (London: SCM Press, 1977), p. 152.
50. Plutarch. Quoted by James Frazer. *The Golden Bough*, pt. 4, vol. 2 (London: Macmillan, [1910], 1936), p. 42.
51. G. L. Gomme in *Funk and Wagnalls' Standard Dictionary of Folklore, Mythology and Legend*. (London: New English Library, 1975), p. 778.
52. Joseph Campbell, *The Hero with a Thousand Faces*. (New York: Pantheon, 1949), p. 256.
53. *Ibid.*, p. 19.
54. Max Müller, *Introduction to the Science of Religion*. (London: Oxford University Press, 1873), p. 352.
55. William Alfred in Foreword to his translation of *Agamemnon*.
56. George Santayana, *Reason in Religion*. (London: Constable, 1923), p. 51.
57. Paul Tillich, "The Religious Symbol" in *Myth and Symbol*, ed. by F. W. Dillistone. (London: S.P.C.K., 1966), p. 22.
58. W. M. Urban, *Humanity and Deity*. (London: George Allen and Unwin, 1951), p. 101.
59. David Burney, *Theoretical Anthropology*. (New York: Columbia University Press, 1953), p. 294.
60. Joseph Campbell, *Myth and Ritual in Christianity*, p. 58.
61. D. F. Strauss, *A New Life of Jesus*. (London and Edinburgh, 1865), vol. 1, p. 214.
62. Baden Powell, *The Order of Nature*. (London, 1859), p. 340.
63. Mircea Eliade, *Myth and Reality*, pp. 5-6.
64. Marianne Nichols, *Man, Myth, and Monument*. (New York: William Morrow, 1975), p. 1.
65. David Bidney, "The Concept of Myth and the Problem of Psychocultural Evolution," p. 27.
66. Reid Bain, "Man—the Myth-Maker." *The Scientific Monthly*, vol. 65, (July 1947), p. 61. It is interesting to compare Bidney's and Bain's views of the relation of myth and science with those of writers who regard myth as a form of proto-science; e.g., H. J. Rose in the *Encyclopedia Americana* (1977), vol. 19, p. 675a states, "Myths are a kind of imaginative precursor of scientific investigation."
67. W. M. Urban, *Language and Reality*, p. 587.
68. John Hick, "Jesus and the World Religions" in *The Myth of God Incarnate*, p. 178.
69. Herbert Mason, "Myth as an 'Ambush of Reality'" in *Myth, Symbol, and Reality*, p. 15.
70. Eric J. Sharpe, *Fifty Key Words: Comparative Religion*. (London: Lutterworth, 1971), p. 43.

71. Hans-Georg Godamer, "Religious and Poetical Speaking" in *Myth, Symbol, and Reality,* p. 92.
72. Rudolf Bultmann, "New Testament and Mythology" in *Kerygma and Myth,* p. 10, note 2.
73. R. G. Collingwood, *Speculum Mentis.* (Oxford: Clarendon, 1924), p. 153.
74. Alan Watts, *Myth and Ritual in Christianity,* p. 7.
75. *Ibid.,* p. 63.
76. G. V. Jones, *Christianity and Myth in the New Testament.* (London: George Allen and Unwin, 1956), p. 35.
77. *Webster's New Dictionary of Synonyms.* (Springfield, Mass.: Merriam, 1973), p. 554.
78. Donald A. Stauffer, "The Modern Myth of the Modern Myth." *English Institute Essays, 1947.* (New York: Columbia University Press, 1948), p. 23.
79. *Encyclopedia of Poetry and Poetics.* (Princeton: Princeton University Press, 1965), p. 538.
80. *Cassell's Modern Guide to Synonyms and Related Words.* ed. by S. I. Hayakawa. Revised by P. J. Fletcher. (London: Cassell, 1984), p. 380.
81. Anton-Hermann Chroust, *Aristotle.* (Notre Dame, Indiana: University of Notre Dame Press, 1973), vol. 1, p. 222.
82. London: Souvenir Press, 1966.
83. *Ibid.,* pp. 2, 6.
84. *Ibid.,* pp. 1, 5, 6.
85. *Ibid.,* pp. 1, 2, 5, 6.
86. *Ibid.,* pp. 2, 7.
87. *Ibid.,* pp. 2, 6.
88. *Ibid.,* p. 6.
89. *Ibid.*
90. *Ibid.,* p. 7.
91. *Ibid.*
92. P. 379.
93. *Ibid.*
94. *Encyclopedia Americana,* vol. 19, 1977, pp. 675a.
95. Boston: Faxon, 1926. Supplement, 1937. Second Supplement, 1952. Similar classifications are found in Gertrude Jobes, *Dictionary of Mythology, Folklore and Symbols* (New York: Scarecrow Press, 1962) and in Norma Ireland, *Index to Fairy Tales, 1949-1972* (Westwood, Mass.: Faxon, 1973.)
96. London: Routledge and Kegan Paul, 1971.
97. *Ibid.,* p. 1.
98. *Ibid.*

99. See "New Testament and Theology" in *Kerygma and Myth*, p. 35.
100. Chicago: University of Chicago Press, 1970.
101. See his *Ideology and Utopia*. London: Kegan Paul, 1936.
102. *Language and Reality*, p. 593.
103. *Myth: Its Meaning and Functions in Ancient and Other Cultures*, p. 2.
104. *Myth and Ritual in Christianity*, p. 64.
105. *Ibid.*, p. 28.
106. P. 778.
107. "Myths, Dreams, and Mysteries" in *Myth and Symbol*, p. 35.

7. On Taking Life Lightly

A generation ago a beloved professor at Drew University was dying. A group of his students came to pay their respects. In the hush of the hospital room one of the students, observing that the sound of breathing had ceased, surmised the professor had died. Another suggested they feel his feet, adding, "No one ever died with warm feet." The dying man opened an eye and commented, "John Hus did."

Although it is not usual to strike a note of humor about one's own death—and especially while in the act of dying—a few have accomplished that feat. For example, John Fisher, the Bishop of Rochester, who had been condemned to die by order of Henry VIII, upon ascending the scaffold threw away his cane saying, "Come on, my feet, you must do these last steps by yourselves. It is a worthy toil." Thomas More stumbled while climbing the gallows. He immediately extended a hand to his executioner and said, "Help me to ascend. I can shift for myself coming down." Egerton Beck described Fisher and More as "two of the finest characters in the whole range of that [i.e., English] history."[1]

One way to take life lightly is to approach death with some degree of levity. I can conceive of five attitudes toward death: Denial, Fear, Defiance, Acceptance, Adventure.

A well-known denial was that of the Epicureans: "When death is, you are not. When you are not, death is." Queen Elizabeth I was one who refused to recognize the fact of death. J. L. Laughton writes of her: "Strong as was her sense of public duty, it failed her here. Her egotism blinded her to the dangers to which her failure to discuss the subject was likely to expose the state. The thought that her dignities must, by the efflux of time, pass to another seems only to have suggested to her the insecurity of her own tenure of them and the coming extinction of her own authority. Such a prospect she could

88

not nerve herself to face."[2] A curious form of denial is to use euphemisms like "moved on," "gone to the heavenly reward," "kicked the bucket," or "passed on" rather than the undesirable word *died*. Samuel Butler advised, "Never have anything to do with the near surviving representative of anyone whose name appears in the death column of the *Times* as having 'passed away.'"

The fear of death is surely the oldest and most universal attitude. Primitive man used charms, fetishes, sacrifices, and ceremonies to alleviate fear. Socrates scoffed at those who feared death, since the fear of death is based on an opinion which could easily be false: ". . . the fear of death is indeed the pretense of wisdom, and not real wisdom, being a pretense of knowing the unknown; and no one knows whether death, which men in their fear apprehend to be the greatest evil, may not be the greatest good."[3]

Defiance of death seems to have a great appeal to those not doing the defying! The "death-defying" act of the trapeze performers at a circus is an example. Bertrand Russell wrote about a Fellow at Cambridge University who defied death in curious forms: he slept in a coffin rather than a bed, and he "used to go out to the college lawns with a spade to cut worms in two, saying as he did so: 'Yah! you haven't got me yet!'"[4] Defiance, however, needs to be modified by the recognition of the inevitability of death. In the words of Reinhold Niebuhr, "Modern man has forgotten that nature intends to kill him, and will succeed in the end."[5]

One of the classic examples of the acceptance of death is found in a letter of Epicurus which begins, "On this truly happy day of my life, as I am at the point of death, I write this to you." David Hume may have had this letter in mind when he stated in his biography which was written while he was on his death bed: ". . . were I to name a period of my life which I should most choose to pass over again, I might be tempted to point to this later period."[6]

Adventure—the most positive attitude that can be taken toward death—is that expressed in *Pilgrim's Progress:* "Now I further saw that betwixt them and the Gate was a River, but there was no Bridge to go over, the River was very deep: at the sight therefore of this River the Pilgrims were much stunned. . . . Then they asked the men if the Waters were all of a depth? They said, No; yet they could not help them in that case, for said they, 'you shall find it deeper or shallower,

89

as you believe in the King of the place.'. . . Then they took courage, and the Enemy was after that as still as a stone, until they were gone over. . . . Thus they got over."[7]

I detect two classes of the ways to take life lightly: the negative and the positive. According to the negative or pessimistic ways life is held to be of too little consequence to be taken seriously. Palladas in the fourth century A.D. advised:

> The world's a stage and life's a toy.
> Dress up, and play your part.
> Put every serious thought aside—
> Or risk a broken heart.

The epitaph on an ancient Greek grave states:

> I was not.
> I became.
> I am not.
> I care not.

The positive or optimistic ways of taking life lightly was well stated by Socrates in his final words to the jury at the Pynx: "The hour of departure has arrived, and we go our ways—I to die, and you to live. Which is better God only knows."[8] Victor Hugo was clearly optimistic when he wrote, "Be like the bird, who halting in his flight on limb too slight, feels it give way beneath him, yet sings, knowing he has wings." A curious mixture of the optimistic and the pessimistic was that of the Christian layman, who when asked by his pastor what he thought would happen to him after death, replied, "Oh, I shall probably go to heaven to enjoy eternal blessedness—but let's not discuss such unpleasant topics." One of the most bittersweet attitudes toward death I have seen is the following which I found on the gravestone of a three-month-old child in Yorkshire:

> So soon I am done for.
> I wonder what I was begun for.

The taking of life and death seriously or lightly is part of what it means to take one's self seriously or lightly. Elbert Hubbard warned against taking one's self seriously. There ought to be an Eleventh

Commandment, he said, viz., "Do not take yourself so damned seriously." There are dimensions of human existence which can be achieved only by basking in the presence of whatever one understands as "The Divine." Religion in this sense is an alternation of commitment and detachment, of duty and relaxation, of seriousness and lightness. There are serious jobs to be done in this world, and to do them well requires heart, strength, will, and mind. There is an obligation to work; but there is also an obligation to rejoice, to play, to praise, to relax. Religious persons are attached to this world. They labor that a kingdom of love might appear on the earth. But they are also detached from this world. They seek a dimension of existence symbolized by the term "eternal life." They are citizens of two worlds, but these worlds are not temporally separated. This is the arena of religious struggle, and it is also the arena of eternal life. Those who have not found the second dimension are like Eeyore, the old grey donkey created by A. A. Milne:

Eeyore, the old grey donkey, stood by the side of the stream, and looked at himself in the water. "Pathetic," he said. "That's what it is. Pathetic."

He turned and walked slowly down the stream for 20 yards, splashed across it, and walked slowly back on the other side. Then he looked at himself in the water again.

"As I thought," he said. "No better from this side. But nobody minds. Nobody cares. Pathetic, that's what it is."

Eeyore takes life seriously. He takes himself seriously. He has no detachment—no sense of humor. If Eeyore possessed detachment, he would recognize that he doesn't look so bad after all, that is, considering the fact that he is an old grey donkey!

To stand, as it were, outside one's self; to criticize, to evaluate, even to laugh at one's self is the mark of a health-minded person. To hold one's hopes, beliefs, and ideals at arm's length on occasion—to step outside the regular routine in order to examine where one is and where one is going—to objectify one's self as subject, as a person, as parent, as spouse, as friend, as a man, as a woman—for this I am pleading. As a permanent state it would be insanity; but as an alternative engaged in on occasion, it is the mark of good health and good religion. William Ernest Hocking argued that the religious life must have the principle of alternation, which for him is a period of close attention to one's work followed by regular intervals of detachment from one's work.

A few examples of taking religion lightly may clarify my meaning. One is the Jewish holiday known as Lag b'Omer, a folk festival placed in the middle of the seven weeks of austerity between Passover and Pentecost. The Omer Days—*Omer* is the Hebrew word meaning "sheaf"—are traditionally the time when it is illegal to marry, to cut the hair, to wear new clothes, to listen to music, or to attend public entertainments. Yet on the thirty-third day of this lenten-like period (the word *Lag* means thirty-three) is a twenty-four hour day when the restrictions are relaxed, a day of singing, dancing, and of shooting with bows and arrows in the woods. A similar day of relaxation and fun in Medieval Christianity was Shrove Tuesday, the day before Ash Wednesday, a day of ribaldry known also as "Pancake Day," since pancakes were enjoyed before people entered a time of self-denial. The Mardi Gras ("meat-eating Tuesday) as celebrated in such cities as Paris and New Orleans is the day of carnival and festivities before the forty weekday period before Easter. In Hinduism the festival known as Holi is a three- or four-day celebration in which the restrictions of caste are not observed. In India it is a time for singing, for lighting bonfires, for dancing around a pole, for throwing colored water on passersby, and even for shouting obscenities at women.

Perhaps the Buddhists of all religionists have been most successful in preserving a note of levity. I once overheard the president of the World's Buddhist Association chastize a Hindu for asking a woman at a cafeteria if the vegetable soup had meat in it, adding, "Why ask? If you don't know, what's the difference?" Perhaps Buddhists go too far when teetotler monks justify drinking whiskey by renaming it "Wisdom Water," or when vegetarians eat pork after asserting that the pig is a "land whale."

Why should we incorporate periods of taking life lightly into our serious life? One reason is that by continual close attention we lose perspective. A man in the midst of a forest cannot see the forest for the trees.

A student in college may lose track of his educational goals through involvement in courses, exams, and papers. A mother of young children may become so involved in meal preparation, house cleaning, and the washing of clothes that she forgets to give her children the friendly encouragement they need. All of us have moments when we feel with Wordsworth,

> The world is too much with us; late and soon,
> Getting and spending, we lay waste our powers.

When we feel like that, we need a change from the normal seriousness of life to moments of detachment, of lightness. Probably no people are more serious about the religious life than the Zen Buddhists. They often meditate for four hours without a stop; some have cut off a hand or arm to convince a teacher that they mean business; the self-immolations of Buddhists in Viet Nam were examples of their seriousness. Yet at certain services the priest steps to the front of the temple and says, "Ladies and gentlemen, let us laugh!" And they laugh!

A second reason for taking life lightly is that the steady pursuit of a goal may stand in the way of that goal. The experience of trying to recall a name is illustrative. The harder one tries, the farther it is from memory. Then, when one relaxes and turns to other matters, the name pops into the mind. The pursuit of certain moral goals is particularly interesting. Take humility. The danger in deliberately cultivating humility is that one will become proud of one's humility—as did Uriah Heep. The same is true for kindness and love. When they are cultivated consciously, rather than flowing from one's being, they tend to become contrived and artificial. I have always liked the story Jesus told about the redeemed who were surprised by their own redemption. "When saw we you hungry and fed you, or naked and clothed you?" they asked. And the reply was "Inasmuch as you have done it unto the least of these, you have done it unto me." Redemption had taken them by surprise. Their goodness was spontaneous. That is genuine virtue.

A third reason for taking life lightly lies in the fact that creative insights come to us in moments of detachment from seriousness. Archimedes' great discovery came to him while he was taking a bath. Newton's insight into gravitation came while he was relaxing under an apple tree. Kekulé formulated the idea of the benzene ring while daydreaming before a fireplace in which he imagined he saw wiggling snakes that seized their own tails. Helmholtz said he had his best ideas not in his laboratory but "when comfortably ascending woody hills in sunny weather." Platt and Baker in a study of the hunch experience in scientific thinking reported that for 232 American scientists, whom they questioned, 83% said they gained their crucial ideas partly as "hunches." We can also think of Thoreau at his door step beside Walden Pond, Wordsworth in his cottage in his beloved lake country, Sibelius in his forest retreat, and Jesus in the wilderness. The great ideas of man—the ideas that have improved man's lot the most—have not been the ideas ground out in committee meetings. They have been the ideas of those who have separated themselves at times to see life from another perspective.

But if one ought to incorporate periods of taking life lightly, how can it be done? One way is through humor. By humor I do not mean that one ought to set for one's self the practice of telling a joke a day! Many so-called "jokes" aren't humorous. Humor is not so much what one says, but what one's attitude is. A man of humor is one who is able to see joy where others cannot. Some have even spoken of the humor of God. For example, Hebrew and Christian mythologies are rather deficient in offering an explanation for God's having created a world. In Hinduism the creation is said to be God's *līlā* (sport or play). God created spontaneously, joyfully, and happily.

A second way is to take one's self lightly. When the Christ said, "He that would save his life shall lose it," was he not saying "He that conscientiously sets himself to preserve himself will discover that self-preservation is self-destruction." The self is something to be spent, not to be preserved. When a friend said to Turgenev, "It seems to me that to put one's self in the second place is the whole significance of life," Turgenev agreed, but added "It seems to me that to discover what to put before one's self in the first place is the whole problem of life." John Woolman, the Quaker who devoted himself to the freeing of the Negro slaves before and during the Civil War, said that he once dreamed that a voice called again and again, "John Woolman. John Woolman. John Woolman." Woolman says that in his dream he tried to answer, "Here I am," but he could not. Then the voice announced, "John Woolman is dead." In a sense Woolman was dead. He had so identified himself with a cause that his self ceased to be a focal point of activity and interest. This, I submit, is the clue to our understanding of immortality. The "self" which we have identified with this body, these personal characteristics, and these memories will be lost in the greater and richer level of existence in which our true identity is revealed.

A third way of taking life lightly is to settle once and for all that despite all the arguments for and against human immortality, there is one indisputable fact about human existence: we do die. We were not consulted about our birth, and we are not consulted about our death. Occasionally we may entertain our fancies with the possibility that our earthly life may be taking place against the backdrop of a wider experience. Thoreau said that our sun is but a morning star. That may be the case. There may be more day to dawn. But hopes of immortality do not eliminate the fact of death. Life cannot be taken lightly until we accept death.

In the fourth century the Emperor Constantine sent his prefect to Bishop Basil of Cappadocia asking the bishop to champion the Emperor's side in a church controversy. But Basil promptly sent back his refusal. Then in a flurry of letters Constantine threatened the bishop with the confiscation of his goods, with exile, and finally with a violent death. Basil replied that he would never yield, that confiscation of goods would not affect him, for he possessed little; that he would be entirely at home with his God in any place of exile; and that a violent death would only hasten his communion with God. Constantine then in exasperation wrote that no one had ever spoken in this form to the Emperor. Basil replied, "Then you never until now have met a Christian bishop." Constantine discovered that he could not touch a man whose life was already forfeit.

The best illustration of what it means to take life lightly may be that of the unnamed person who said to Augustine, "If I were never to die, it would be well; but if I am ever to die, why not now?"[9] Augustine's own dying words minimized the significance of dying: "He will not be great who thinks it a great matter that wood and stone fall and mortals die."

NOTES

1. "The English Martyrs." *The Dublin Review*, vol. 187, 1930, p. 31.
2. *The Cambridge Modern History*, vol. 3, p. 359.
3. Plato, *The Apology* 29A. Jowett translation.

4. "Stoicism and Mental Health" in *In Praise of Idleness and Other Essays.* (New York: Simon and Schuster, 1972), p. 247.
5. *The Nature and Destiny of Man,* vol. 1. (New York: Scribners, 1941), p. 191.
6. In this connection one might examine the following studies of Elizabeth Kubler-Ross: *Questions and Answers on Death and Dying* (New York: Macmillan, 1974), *Coping with Death and Dying* (New York: Macmillan, 1980), and *Living with Death and Dying* (New York: Macmillan, 1981). See also Harold Orlans' study of 530 statements on death from a questionaire made in May 1942 and recorded in the London Files of Mass-Observation. "Some Attitudes Toward Death." (*Diogenes,* no. 19, fall 1957), pp. 73-91.
7. See also Virginia Moore, *Ho for Heaven.* (New York: E. P. Dutton, 1946.)
8. Plato, *The Apology* 42A. Jowett translation.
9. Possidus, *Santi Augustini Vita,* chap. 27.

8. The Roots of the Whole

Fritjof Capra in *The Tao of Physics* argues that the Cartesian dualism of matter and spirit and the mechanistic world view have been both beneficial and detrimental. They made possible the development of classical physics and technology, but they have many diverse consequences for Western civilization. Capra writes, "It is fascinating to see that twentieth-century science, which originated in the Cartesian split and in the mechanistic world view, and which indeed only became possible because of such a view, now overcomes this fragmentation and leads back to the idea of unity expressed in the early Greek and Eastern philosophies."[1] He writes also, "The roots of physics, as of all Western science, are to be found in the sixth century B.C. in a culture where science, philosophy and religion were not separated."[2] In this paper I wish to call attention to these wholistic roots. Some of them are, as Capra says, in the Greek philosophers of the sixth century B.C., but some are found in later Western philosophers, and, in addition, there are similar roots in Eastern philosophy.

The popularity of Capra's book should not blind us to the fact that other Western scientists had already noted the need to move toward an organic or mystical view of the world. For example, Wolfgang Pauli in a lecture entitled "Science and Western Thought" given in Copenhagen in 1955 closed with these words, "Since the seventeenth century the activities of the human spirit have been strictly classified in separate compartments. But in my view the attempt to eliminate such distinctions by a combination of rational understanding and the mystical experience of unity obeys the explicit or implicit imperative of our own contemporary age."[3]

The earliest roots in Greek thought are found in the eighth century rather than the sixth, as Capra states. Hesiod held that before the appearance of earth and sky as separate entities they were

97

one. A gap appeared and the one became two with a nothingness between. The agency of separation is not named. Among the Babylonians the agent was Marduk who killed the great mother goddess Tiamat and split her into two halves—earth and sky. The myth of creation by splitting an original unity into halves was so ancient in the fifth century B.C. that Euripides referred to it as a tradition handed down: "Not from me but from my mother comes the tale how earth and sky were once one form, but being separated, brought forth all things, sending into light trees, birds, wild beasts, those nourished by the salt sea and the race of mortals."[4] The myth of the breaking of the primordial unity among the Greeks may have been due to opposing male and female principles in the original unity.

Although the Milesian philosophers—Thales, Anaximander, and Anaximenes—turned away from the mythopoetic speculations of Hesiod, they felt the necessity of dealing with the problem of the One and the Many. What is the basic stuff from which all things have come and which remains as their essential nature, and by what process does the One become Many? The basic stuff (*Urstoff* in German), said Thales, is water. Water is the only one of the four elements—earth, air, fire, and water—which can appear in the three basic forms: solid, liquid, and vapor. Anaximenes thought it was air; Anaximander, exhibiting great imagination by stepping outside the four elements, speculated that it had to be something without limits. So he called it the Unlimited, the Infinite, the Unbounded, *to apeirōn*.

The problem of many-ing, for these sixth-century Greek philosophers, was the problem of change: change of place, change of quality, change of quantity, and the change of coming-into-being and passing-into-non-being. Thales said the efficient cause of change is within, thus rejecting the common notion that earthly existence is a marionette show in which the gods pull the strings. Although he referred to these inner moving causes as "gods," that was only a Greek way of saying that they are eternal. Anaximander said the changes of rest to motion, cold to hot, and one to many are the inherent efforts of opposites to overcome the injustice of their opposition. Change is the compensation which attempts to resolve the opposition of hot-cold and wet-dry—and also the indeterminateness inherent in the fact that the One which is Totality contains all opposites. Axaminenes said change is produced by condensation and rarefaction; that is, the transformation of the single substance is purely quantitative. Air rarified becomes fire; air condensed becomes water; and air condensed still more becomes earth. He added, "The rest are produced from these." This means that all individual and particular things that come into being come by the same process, i.e., dilation and compression. All come from the *Urstoff*, and all remain *Urstoff* in nature.

The root of the view of modern physics that atomic particles are processes rather than objects is clearly the view of Heraclitus, the Ionian philosopher who was obsessed by the notion of change. One cannot step into the same river twice, he said. His student Cratylus outdid him, saying one cannot step into the same river once. Yet a more careful examination of what Heraclitus taught reveals that we may have misunderstood him. It is the water that is processed and pluralized; the river is the same. According to Arius Didymus what Heraclitus actually said was, "Upon those who step into the same rivers flow other and yet other waters."[5] He also referred to an everlasting fire which is perpetually and predictably transformed into the myriad of things. Those who know only the many have polymathy (a knowledge of particulars), and such knowledge does not make one wise. Wisdom is the understanding of the Whole which appears in and through the things. According to the Greek poet Archilochus, "The fox knows many things, the hedgehog only one— the one big one." Man is the being who can perceive the One in the Many, who can deduce the reality of the One from his experience of the Many.

Parmenides, like Śaṅkara, contended that only the Whole is real. There are two ways of inquiry: (1) the way of truth, the way of how it is and how it is not possible for it not to be, and (2) the way of opinion, the way of how it is not, and how it is necessary for it not to be. The subject matter of the former is Being as unbegotten, imperishable, whole, immovable, and complete. Being cannot at any one time be and at another time not be, since Being is eternally now, all at once, and continuous. The subject matter of the latter is begotten, perishable, part, movable, and incomplete. The Whole is real in itself; the Part is real only as derived from the Whole. In the language of Advaita the Whole is *sat*; the Part is *māyā*. Parmenides and Śaṅkara had the same difficulty in their views of the relation of Whole and

99

Part. It is not enough to say that unity, singleness, wholeness, and simplicity make room for diversity, account for the many, or explain our human experience of particulars. Rather it must be shown that unity (singleness, wholeness, simplicity) must become (emanate in, yield, create, fashion, produce) diversity (plurality, parts, the many) in order to become the totality which it essentially is.

Śaṅkara needed a Rāmānuja to correct his overzealous efforts to affirm unity and denigrate plurality. The individual selves are not *māyā* countered Rāmānuja; they are the Many without which the One would not be the All. Plato needed an Aristotle to warn him against the dangers of separation (*chōris*) of the Forms from the particulars, of Good from things that are good, and of knowledge from the life of sensation and experience. "No universal can exist apart from its concrete individuals."[6] Likewise I think Capra in places in his book needs someone to remind him that unity is the unity of parts. He forgets that chapter ten of his book is titled "The Unity of All Things" rather than "Unity." In this chapter he writes, "In ordinary life, we are not aware of this unity of all things, but divide the world into separate objects and events. This division is useful and necessary to cope with our everyday experiences, but it is not a fundamental feature of reality. It is an abstraction devised by our discriminating and categorizing intellect. To believe that our abstract concepts of separate 'things' and 'events' are realities of nature is an illusion."[7] Capra in describing the world of separate things and events as "illusion" falls into the same error that Plato made in denying existence to particular ontological objects and that Śaṅkara made in reducing the individual self (*jīva*) to the condition known as *māyā*. Capra corrects himself later in the book when he states that no part of the universe qua part is fundamental.[8] It is one thing to state as he does, "All natural phenomena are ultimately interconnected, and in order to explain any one of them we need to understand all the others, which is obviously impossible."[9] It is quite a different thing to claim that the world of natural phenomena is an "illusion." What Capra ought to have stated is that the Whole and the Part are so interconnected that Part without Whole is not Part, and that Whole without Part is not Whole.

The roots of the whole are easy to indicate in Indian thought. The Brahman—the integrated and integrating concept in Upaniṣadic

100

thought—is well known. But what is not so well known is that plurality was not ignored in this early Indian speculation; e.g., the seer in the *Īśa Upaniṣad* praises the one who sees all beings in the *Ātman*, and the *Ātman* in all beings. The *Taittirīya Upaniṣad* contains the following:

> He desired: 'Would that I were many! Let me procreate myself!' He performed austerity. Having performed austerity he created this whole world, whatever there is here. Having created it, into it, he entered. Having entered it, he became both the actual and the yon, both the defined and the undefined, both the based and the non-based, both the conscious and the unconscious, both the real and the false. As the real, he became whatever there is here. That is what they call the real.[10]

And the following is found in the *Chandogya Upaniṣad*:

> In the beginning . . . this world was just Being, one only, without a second. To be sure, some people say: "In the beginning this world was Non-being, one only, without a second; from that Non-being Being was produced." . . . On the contrary . . . in the beginning this world was just Being, one only, without a second. It bethought itself: "Would that I were many! Let me procreate myself!"[11]

John Bowker has written, "Suffering is the result of introducing duality into a non-dualistic situation. Existence is a unity. All that is, is an aspect or manifestation of Being-itself, Brahman. To break down that unity is to introduce tension and conflict and strife."[12] Usually Bowker means by "duality" the taking of two points of view of a perceived or conceived situation[13] or the contrast between pain and pleasure,[14] and by "dualism" two eternally opposing on-tological principles.[15] But here he slips and uses the term "dualism" to denote introducing twoness into the concept of Brahman. But, if Brahman is to designate "all that is,"—as he states—then Brahman must also designate the full possibilities. The many-ing of Brahman does not "break down that unity" and "introduce tension and con-flict and strife." Rather it is the explication of what it means for Brahman to be "all that is." Bowker writes a few pages later, "Re-lease is only possible when the parts are *seen* to be parts, and Brahman is realised as the sole truth."[16] He would be more accurate were he to state, "Release is only possible when the Brahman is understood to be the whole which necessarily includes the 'parts' as the necessary manifestation of the fullness of Brahman."

Wholistic concepts are also found in the *Rig Veda*. One root of the whole in the *Rig Veda* was the tendency to cluster the gods into groups such as the Maruts, the Aśvins, and the Rudras. But in addition there were the Vasus, i.e., eight deities, attendants upon Indra who were the collective personification of natural phenomena—water, the pole-star, the moon, earth, wind, fire, dawn, and light. Later the entire pantheon was referred to by terms such as Viśvedevas, Viśvas, and Viśvāmitras. Henotheism, Max Müller's term for the Vedic tendency to make different gods in the pantheon supreme, also was a monistic tendency. At the time of sacrifice to one god it was not uncommon to make this god supreme—the other gods being but powers or attributes to the one given top billing in the ritual. Henotheism has been called "opportunistic monotheism" and "a sort of mitigated polytheism," but I think the tendency needs recognition as a root of the whole in Vedic ritualism. Another root in Vedism was the interesting experiments in stepping outside the traditional polytheism to find a cosmic creator, a one responsible for the all. Thus we find such terms as Viśvakarman (the world maker), Hiraṇyagarbha (the Golden Embryo), Brahmaṇaspati and Bṛihaspati (the Lord of Prayer), and Prajāpati (the Lord of Creation). Sometimes the *deva* singled out as transcendent to all *devas* was called Aditi (the Free or the Boundless). The connotation of Aditi was about the same as *to apeirōn* in Anaximander's speculation. Aditi was thought of as boundless space and as the boundless heaven. (One of the rare occasions where sky is female and earth is male.) Aditi was also known as *deva-matro* (the mother of the gods). Other symbols of wholeness in early Indian thought were Tat (That), Tat Ekam (That One), Sat (Being), Ka (The Who), and Vac (Sound). Sound appears as Vācas-pati, Brihas-pati, and Brāhmaṇas-pati (all meaning the Lord of Holy Utterance). But the most important root of the whole in the Vedas, I believe, is the concept of *Rita*. Literally, *Rita* means "the course of things." It was the uniformity of nature, the ordered course of things, the universal and eternal natural law. Religiously it was that which all gods dispensed; metaphysically it has some resemblance to Plato's Good as the standard of perfection and the dispenser of good in all things, to *Maat* (justice in ancient Egyptian thought), and, of course, to *Logos*. It was described poetically as "the father of all." *Rita*, like *moira* among the Greeks, was a cosmic order which even the *devas* could not transgress, e.g., "The dawn follows the path of *Rita*, the right path; as if she knew them before. She never oversteps the regions. The sun follows the path of *Rita*."[17]

The *Bhagavad Gītā* in its uniquely confusing manner also refers to the many-ing of the whole; e.g., in chapter 9, verses 4, 5, and 6, Lord Kṛṣṇa speaking vis-à-vis Brahman says to Arjuna:

> All beings rest in Me,
> And I do not rest in them.
>
> And yet beings do not rest in Me:
> Behold My divine mystery!
> Supporter of beings, and not resting in them,
> Is My Self, that causes things to be.
>
> So all beings
> Abide in Me.[18]

I interpret this passage to mean that while all beings are ontologically dependent on the Brahman, the Brahman-qua-Absolute does not depend upon the existence of beings, although the Brahman-qua-Totality does necessitate manifestation in beings. In Tillichean terms the Ground of Being would not be *Ground* were there no things of which It is Ground.

Aurobindo was one of the few Indian philosophers of this century who, while identifying himself with the Advaita Vedānta tradition, insisted that pluralization is an ontic necessity of the Brahman. This may be one of the reasons why Aurobindo is often described by Indian philosophers as a religionist rather than a philosopher. I rediscovered this evaluation in 1983 while I was a Visiting Professor of Philosophy at Jadvapur University in Calcutta and a participant in an International Seminar on Aurobindo. Again I was informed by some that Aurobindo was a quasi-philosopher. Advaita philosophers do not like to be confronted with the view that many-ing is an element of oneness. Aurobindo was a yogi who insisted that the path from the One to the Many is just as regal as the path from the Many to the One. The conflict between the Advaitins (the non-dualists) and the Viśiṣṭadvaitins (the modified nondualists) takes strange forms in modern India. During my first year in India (1959) I had to move from North India to South India because libraries in the north would not stock their shelves with materials on Rāmānuja, the twelfth-century philosopher who taught the eternity of the individual self. And in 1970, while on a bus trip west of Madras with a group of Indian philosophers, I was amused to hear the followers of Śankara make unflattering remarks about a follower of Rāmānuja who got off at Conjeeveram to pay respects to the memory of Rāmānuja.

After this excursion into the roots of the whole in Indian thought, I want to return to the Greeks—especially to the Pythagoreans, those puzzling poetic mathematicians whose influence is still puzzling.

The ancient Pythagoreans formulated a list of important general notions in the form of ten pairs of contrarieties or cognates which, I believe, are consistently misrepresented by historians of philosophy as ideas connected by a conjunction, e.g., limit *and* unlimited, odd *and* even. Such a listing ignores the metaphysical significance of the list. I submit that the ten should be listed as follows:

1. Limited without unlimited is not limited.
2. Odd without even is not odd.
3. One without plurality is not one.
4. Right without left is not right.
5. Male without female is not male.
6. Resting without moving is not resting.
7. Straight without curved is not straight.
8. Light without darkness is not light.
9. Good without bad is not good.
10. Square without oblong is not square.

I find the following pairs in Capra's *The Tao of Physics*—stated again according to my formulation:

Destructible without indestructible is not destructible.[19]
Matter-as-continuous without matter-as-discontinuous is not matter-as-continuous.[20]
Space without time is not space.[21]
Waves without particles are not waves.[22]
Matter without energy is not matter.[23]
Rest without motion is not rest.[24]

Particles without antiparticles are not particles.[25]
Existence without nonexistence is not existence.[26]

Capra states that "in atomic physics we have to go even beyond the concepts of existence and non-existence."[27] This calls to mind that almost untranslatable passage in *The Republic*[28] in which Plato says the Good is not a thing in *presbeia* (rank, dignity) and in *dunamis* (strength, might, ability, power). Going beyond existence and nonexistence is exactly what Advaita Vedāntists do in Four-Corner Negation by stating that the most positive statement about Nirguṇa Brahman is that it is not true that Brahman exists, that Brahman does not exist, that Brahman both exists and does not exist, and that Brahman neither exists nor does not exist. In the Western theological tradition Paul Tillich argued that God does not exist, since God is the ground of being—and the ground of being does not exist. Tillich's words are, "He is being-itself beyond essence and existence."[29] However, when Tillich writes, "The ground of being cannot be found within the totality of beings"[30] I wish he had been more careful. He should have added: "The ground of being without plurality of beings would not be the ground of being."

If the Pythagoreans had known the *Tao Teh Ching* they could have added to their list "Yang without Yin is not the Tao." They should have turned upon Parmenides by arguing that being without nonbeing is not being, that the One cannot be One without a Many, that the "how it is" without the "how it is not" is not how it is. Although the statement sounds oxymoronic, Parmenides and Śaṅkara must be reminded that being without nonbeing is not being. One of the best statements I know of this position is that of Frithjof Schoun in his book *Language of the Self*: ". . . in a certain sense *Māyā* represents the possibility for Being of not being. The All-Possibility must by definition and on pain of contradiction include its own impossibility. It is in order not to be, that Being incarnates in the multitude of souls; it is in order not to be, that the ocean squanders itself in myriads of flecks of foam. . . . Nothing is external to absolute Reality; the world is therefore a kind of internal dimension of Brahman. But Brahman is without relativity; thus the world is a necessary aspect of the absolute necessity of Brahman. Put in another way, relativity is an aspect of the Absolute. . . . If the existence of the relative were excluded from possibility, the Absolute would not be the Absolute. . . . Diversity, for its part, is but the inverse of the Infinity, or of the All-Possibility, of Brahman."[31]

Capra makes the following statement about ultimate reality— Brahman, Dharmakaya (Body of Being), Tathata (Suchness), or Tao—"[It] cannot be separated from its multiple manifestations. It is central to its very nature to manifest itself in myriad forms which come into being and disintegrate, transforming themselves into one another without end."[32] This is a good statement, but it needs improvement. The "myriad forms" come into being not only because it is the "nature" of Ultimate Reality but also because it is necessary. The necessity is that Ultimate Reality is also Absolute Reality, and, to be absolute, pluralization is required. Ultimate Reality must become all that is possible, or it is not the Absolute. This is the insight of Schuon.

One of the fine contributions of Aurobindo to Indian thought is the restoration of Matter (the nature of which is plurality) to a non-*māyā* position and of Spirit (the nature of which is unity) to a process matrix. In Aurobindo's system Matter is Spirit devoluting and Spirit is Matter evoluting. Devolution-evolution is a cosmic dance, a *līlā* (sport). The cycle of devolution-evolution is a magnificent cosmic *kalpa* similar to Heraclitus' upward and downward path which Heraclitus described in his typical paradoxical manner as "the same." Aurobindo's devolution-evolution relationship of the One and the Many offers far more insight on the Upaniṣadic mantra *tat tvam asi* than does the *sat-māyā* interpretation of Śaṅkara. Brahman without *māyā* is not Totality—Brahman without *māyā* is not Brahman—and, even more strikingly stated, Brahman without *māyā* is a nothing.

My references to Schuon and Aurobindo lead me to question Capra's observation: "In the Eastern view . . . the division of nature into separate objects is not fundamental and any such objects have a fluid and ever-changing character."[33] I have been arguing that the pluralization of Nirguṇa Brahman (or *Saccidānanda*, to use the term preferred by Aurobindo) is fundamental to the total reality (or real totality) of Brahman. Brahman would not be the All if some possibilities were not actualized. And, secondly, I argue that having "a fluid and ever-changing character" is not a deficiency, inasmuch as change or process is inherent in the value (*ānanda*) of *Saccidānanda*. This, I take it, is the wisdom in the concept of Trimurti: Creation (Brahmā) requires both Preservation (Viṣṇu) and Destruction (Śiva).

The last root of the Whole and Part in the Western philosophical tradition to which I wish to direct attention comes from Plotinus who in the third century of the Common Era offered a Platonism which took Plato's Good seriously. The One (his term for Plato's Good) is that from which proceed "manifoldness, duality, and number." Plotinus asks, "Why did the One not remain within itself, why did it emit that manifoldness that we find to characterize Being and which we seek to trace back to the One?" He answers, "Everything that has arrived at its point of perfection becomes productive. That which is eternally perfect is eternally productive."[34] Since the One is perfect, it must be productive—eternally productive. Plotinus says much the same elsewhere: "Now when anything else comes to perfection we see that it produces, and does not endure to remain by itself, but makes something else. . . . How then could the Most Perfect, the First Good, the Power of all things, remain in Itself as if It grudged Itself or was unable to produce? How would it then still be the Principle?"[35] But what is the necessity which results in the One manying? He flatly denies that it is the necessity of the willing of the One. He says it is for the good of the One since the good of the Whole consists chiefly in the variety of its parts.

A rational world—which is the kind of world implied by the nature of the Plotinian One—must exhibit all degrees of beings however imperfect. The One cannot be the One unless it is "full" (Plotinus' own word). It is not merely that a world with both One and Many is the best of all possible worlds, as Leibniz was later to say, but also that the One without the Many would not be the One. This, which is known as the Principle of Plentitude—plus the Principle of Continuity and the Principle of Gradation—constitutes the Great Chain of Being, the integrative insight which held Western culture together for two thousand years. Since 1859 (the date of the publication of Darwin's *The Origin of Species*) the West has been searching—thus far unsuccessfully—for an integrative idea which will do for a dynamic world what the Great Chain of Being did for a static world.

Pierre Teilhard de Chardin and Martin Buber are two Western philosophical mystics who have attempted to formulate an integration of Whole and Part adequate for a post-Darwinian world. Chardin postulated an Omega Point in the cosmic future, when through the noosphere, i.e., the sphere of mind, the cosmos will reach collectively a point of convergence, and all will be one. Martin Buber's concern, especially in his later years, was the problem of unity in multiplicity. This problem for him, in the words of Robert E. Wood, was the problem of gathering into unity "the multiple polarities he had noted earlier: spirit and matter, matter and form, being and becoming, reason and will, positivity and negativity. He accomplished this by introducing his own polarity, I-Thou and I-It, and then developing its implication in a way which integrates the traditional polarities."[36]

I close with a reference to Goethe's *Faust*. At the opening of the work Faust celebrates: "How everything moves toward the whole; each in the other works and lives, like seraphs climbing up and down, passing to one another golden buckets! On blessed fragrant wings pressing from heaven through earth, all sounding through the All with harmony!" Mephistopheles tempers Faust's enthusiasm by reminding him, "I am part of the part that first was all." In other words, evil is part of the whole. In the encomium of the whole do not forget the role of even the meanest or seemingly undesirable part. *Pars pro toto* (a part can stand for the whole) because each part is integral with the whole.

NOTES

1. *The Tao of Physics*. (Boulder, Colorado: Shambhala Publications, 1977), p. 10. The fourth lecture titled "The One and the Many" in William James' *Pragmatism* contains James' assessment: "I have come, by long brooding on it, to consider the problem of the One and the Many the most central of all philosophic problems."
2. *Ibid.*, p. 6.
3. Quoted by Robert Jungk in *Brighter than a Thousand Suns*. Trans. by James Cleugh. (New York: Harcourt Brace Jovanovich, Inc., 1958), p. 341.
4. Fragment 484.

5. See John Robinson, *An Introduction to Early Greek Philosophy.* (New York: Houghton Mifflin Co., 1968), p. 91.

6. *Metaphysics* 1040 b 25. My translation.

7. *The Tao of Physics*, p. 117.

8. *Ibid.*, p. 280.

9. *Ibid.*, p. 277.

10. 2. 6. Robert Ernest Hume translation.

11. 6. 2. 1-4. Hume translation.

12. *Problems of Suffering in Religions of the World.* (London: Cambridge University Press, 1980), p. 211.

13. *Ibid.*

14. *Ibid.*, p. 215.

15. *Ibid.*, pp. 52, 119, 203, 205.

16. *Ibid.*, p. 214.

17. *Rig Veda* 1. 24. 8.

18. Franklin Edgerton translation.

19. P. 134.

20. *Ibid.*

21. *Ibid.*

22, *Ibid.*, p. 136.

23. *Ibid.*, p. 137.

24. *Ibid.*

25. *Ibid.*, pp. 212-13.

26. *Ibid.*, p. 137.

27. *Ibid.*, p. 275.

28. 509B.

29. *Systematic Theology*, vol. 1. (Chicago: University of Chicago Press, 1951), p. 205.

30. *Ibid.*

31. Madras: (Ganesh and Co., 1959), pp. 22-23.

32. *The Tao of Physics*, p. 175.

33. *Ibid.*, p. 10.

34. *Enneads* 5. 1. 6. Trans. by Joseph Katz.

35. *Ibid.*, 5. 4. 1. Trans. by A. H. Armstrong.

36. *Martin Buber's Ontology.* (Evanston: Northwestern University Press, 1969), p. 117.

9. The Split Brain and East-West Understanding

A new classification of human beings offers promising insights into the differences of Eastern and Western people. This grows out of observations of and experiments on the human brain. Physiologists have long known that the brain of higher mammals is double. They have also known that the left hemisphere of the brain controls the right side of the body, and that the right hemisphere of the brain controls the left side of the body. Damage to the left side of the skull may result in paralysis of the right arm and/or leg, and damage to the right side of the skull may paralyze the left arm and/or leg. An isthmus of nerve connects the right and left sides of the cerebrum. This connecting link is known as the corpus callosum.

The neurologist Hughlings Jackson noted in 1864 that damage to the left hemisphere of the human brain often interfered with language ability, and damage to the right hemisphere disturbed spatial awareness, musical ability, recognition of other people, and awareness of one's own body. He referred to the left side of the brain as the locus of expression, audio-articular activities, and propositioning, and to the right side as the locus of perception, retino-ocular activities, and visual imagery.

In the early 1950s two scientists at the University of Chicago, Ronald E. Myers and R. W. Sperry, discovered that when the connection between the two halves of the brain is cut, each hemisphere functions independently as if it were a complete brain. The phenomenon was first observed in a cat in which not only the brain but also the optic chiasma—the crossover of the optic nerve—was severed. Visual information from the left eye was dispatched only to the left side of the brain, and information from the right eye was dispatched only to the right side of the brain. The cat, working on a problem with one eye, could respond normally and learn to perform

110

a task. But when that eye was covered and the same problem was presented to the other eye, the cat, evidencing no recognition of the problem, had to relearn the solution.

In 1961 P. J. Vogel and Joseph E. Bogan of the California College of Medicine performed a complete commissurotomy—the cutting of all interconnections between the two hemispheres of the brain—on a war veteran who was suffering from uncontrollable epilepsy, in the hope that the seizures could be confined to one half of the brain.[1]

In 1969 Bogan published an article entitled "The Other Side of the Brain: An Appositional Mind" in which he referred to the left hemisphere of the brain as propositional and the right as appositional.[2] His terminology had been preceded by the following:[3]

Left Hemisphere	Right Hemisphere	Scientist and Date of Naming
Linguistic	Visual	(Weisenberg and McBride, 1935)
Storage	Executive	(Anderson, 1951)
Symbolic	Imaginative	(Humphrey and Zangwill, 1951)
Education of relations	Education of correlates	(McFie and Piercy, 1952)
Verbal	Perceptual	(Milner, 1958)
Discrete	Diffuse	(Semmes, Weinstein, Ghent, Teuber, 1960)
Symbolic	Visuospatial	(Zangwill, 1961)
Linguistic	Pre-verbal	(Hécaen, Ajuriaguerra, Angelergues, 1963)
Logical or analytic	Synthetic perceptual	(Levy-Agresti and Sperry, 1968)

Robert E. Ornstein in *The Nature of Human Consciousness* wrote, "A major thesis of this book is that two major modes of consciousness exist in Man, the intellectual and its complement, the intuitive. Contemporary science, (and, indeed, much of Western culture) has predominantly emphasized the intellectual mode, and has filtered out rich sources of evidence: meditation, 'mysticism,' non-ordinary reality, the influence of 'the body' on 'the mind.' In part, this book is intended to open inquiry into that inelegant, tacit, 'other' side of ourselves."[4]

A fuller listing of the functions of the left and the right hemispheres of the human brain would look like this:

111

Left Hemisphere	*Right Hemisphere*
rational	intuitive
scientific	artistic
prosaic	poetic
utilitarian	aesthetic
linear	cyclical
discursive	meditative
critical	creative
temporal	spatial
intellectual	intuitive
analytic	synthetic
partitive	integrative
factual	evaluative
ontological	axiological
gnostic	mystical
impassive	emotional
realistic	idealistic

Perhaps the simplest and best terminology is to refer to the verbal left brain and the nonverbal right brain.

Some studies have indicated that the direction a person glances when solving a problem is determined by the kind of problem, e.g., when asked questions of a verbal-analytical nature, such as "What is 144 divided by 6, and then multiplied by 7?" or "What does the proverb 'A few swallows do not make a summer day' mean?", more eye movements are made to the right; whereas when asked questions involving spatial mentation, e.g., "Which way does Jefferson face on the nickel coin and Lincoln face on the penny?" or "What is the relationship of the letter E to the letter V on the keys of a typewriter?", more eye movements are made to the left. Other studies have indicated that lawyers presenting a brief in court tend to glance to the right, and dancers rising on their points tend to glance to the left.[5]

The proclivity of individuals to stress the intellect to the exclusion of emotions, or emotions to the exculsion of the intellect, may be described as a form of self-imposed commissurotomy. Marilyn Ferguson in her book *The Aquarian Conspiracy* observes, "Without the benefit of a scalpel, we perform split-brain surgery on ourselves. We isolate heart and mind. Cut off from the fantasy, dreams, intuitions, and holistic processes of the right brain, the left is sterile. And the right brain, cut off from integration with its organizing partner, keeps recycling its emotional charge. Feelings are damned, perhaps to work private mischief in fatigue, illness, neurosis, a pervasive sense of something wrong, something missing—a kind of cosmic homesickness."[6]

The discovery of the split brain of man suggests that C. P. Snow's dichotomy of two cultures may have been hasty and superficial. Jerome S. Bruner in his book *On Knowing: Essays for the Left Hand* writes, "I find myself a little out of patience with the alleged split between 'the two cultures,' for the two are not simply external ways of life, one pursued by humanists, and the other by scientists. They are ways of living with one's own experience."[7] Ornstein, however, as noted above, believes that the split brain helps us understand East and West. The Western mode of consciousness is analytic, rational, verbal, linear, and scientific; the Eastern mode of consciousness is holistic, intuitive, nonrational, nonverbal, emotional, mystical, and religious.

There are at least three errors in making a precise listing of mental and psychological characteristics of Easterners and Westerners. One error is the assumption that terms like idealistic, realistic, mystical, and religious have the same philosophical and technical meanings in the East and the West. Filmer S. C. Northrop very wisely avoided this error in his study *The Meeting of East and West*[8] by proposing a new technical terminology for comparative philosophy. According to Northrop a theory of any kind is a body of propositions and a body of propositions is a set of concepts. A concept is a term to which a meaning has been assigned. There are two ways in which meaning may be assigned. One is by appeal to data given immediately, e.g., blue as a color sensed by the eye and the optic nerve. The other is by appeal to theoretical postulation within a deductive system, e.g., blue as a certain wave-length in electromagnetic theory. Northrop called the former "concepts by intuition" and the latter "concepts by postulation." His contention was that in the Western world concepts by postulation are given priority and concepts by intuition are given a secondary position, whereas in the Eastern world the reverse is the case. In the 1939 East-West Philosophers' Conference at the University of Hawaii Northrop argued that "by independent developments in the East and in the West a new and more comprehensive philoso-phy is being made articulate in which the basic intuited factor discovered long ago in the Orient is being combined with the newly conceived postulated composition of the nature of things, necessi-tated by the recent revolutionary scientific discoveries of the West."9 He foresaw a "new philosophy" including both concepts by which East and West would be "combined into a single world civilization, the richer and better because it includes in complementary harmony with balanced emphasis the most profound and mature insights of each."10

Romano Guardini in *The End of Modern Man*11 made a division similar to Northrop's "concepts by intuition" and "concepts by postulation." The "human man," he said, has an elastic harmo-nious, direct relationship with nature; the "non-human man" has only an indirect relationship. The latter knows things intellectually and scientifically. The old immediateness is gone. His relations with nature are transmitted by mathematics or by instruments. Nature is ominous and distant. Nature has ceased for "non-human man" to be a "natural nature" and has become a "non-natural nature." Nature has become a world of symbols rather than a world of experience.

The second error of Ornstein's list of the Western and the Eastern modes of consciousness—and to a lesser extent of Northrop's two concepts—is the failure to note there is variety among both Eastern and Western peoples. Plotinus and William Blake, e.g., were right-brain persons, stressing concepts by intuition. Confucius was a left-brain person, stressing concepts by postulation. Northrop had diffi-culty fitting Confucius and the Neo-Confucians into his concept by intuition group, admitting that in Confucianism "the concept of the indeterminate intuited manifold moves into the background of thought."12 Zen Buddhists, on the other hand, fit nicely into his thesis that Eastern peoples stress concepts by intuition, and most Western physicists fit his claim that Western peoples stress concepts by postulation. I can think of no single characteristic which would differentiate Eastern and Western peoples. One candidate might be "Occidentals are more mechanically skilled than are Orientals." This I might support by my memory of seeing high octane gasoline being delivered by oxcarts in Indian airports to Western built planes. But my supporting evidence is weakened by another memory, that of seeing Indian village homes in which the floors are made of concrete beautifully dyed in permanent shades of red and green by mixing dry dyes into the mortar, a technique which an American contractor assured me is not possible!

A third error, as we shall note later, is in supporting that all human beings, whether Eastern or Western, make verbal discriminations in the left hemisphere of the brain and emotional, artistic, and spatial discriminations in the right hemisphere of the brain. The error lies in ignoring the influence right-handedness and left-handedness may have on the functioning of the two hemispheres of the brain. Does the dominant brain hemisphere determine which hand is dominant, or does the dominant hand determine brain hemisphere dominance?

Ornstein correctly calls attention to one Asian way of thought and action which has achieved a remarkable integration of the intellectual and the intuitive. This is the ancient Chinese way of integrating the *yang*, i.e., the light, active, aggressive, penetrating, primal power, and the *yin*, i.e., the dark, yielding, receptive, absorbing, primal power. *Yang-yin* represents heaven in relation to earth, nature to spirit, time to space, male to female, mountain to valley, rock to stream, spring-summer to autumn-winter, positive to negative. The two are not opposed in a destructive manner. The earliest expression of this duality in China is to be found in the *Pa Kua* (Eight Trigrams). It consists of combinations of straight lines arranged in a circle. In Chinese mythology the first to have formed the *Pa Kua* was a culture hero known as Ku Hsi. In the Eight Trigrams a solid straight line called *yang-yao* symbolizes the male or positive principle, and a broken straight line called *yin-yao* symbolizes the female or negative principle. The various combinations of solid and broken lines suggest the harmonious opposition of *yang* and *yin* in the eight fundamental elements of the universe, viz., Heaven and Earth, Water and Fire, Thunder and Sun, Marsh and Mountain. Harmonious opposition is an opposition which enhances rather than destroys. A good example is sweet-sour in Chinese cooking. The Eight Trigrams appear with the symbol of creation in the center, i.e., two intertwining "fish" forming a perfect circle. *Yang* is the red "fish" with a black eye and *yin* is the black "fish" with a red eye, a reminder that *yang* and *yin* are not contradictory opposites but necessary bipolarities. The *Pa Kua* is thus a reminder that where Western thinkers see opposites like

115

good and evil, form and matter, and God and man, Eastern thinkers tend to see complementaries in necessary juxtaposition.

WATER

FIRE

Later the Eight Trigrams were combined to form the Sixty-four Hexagrams, a more complicated chart used to account for all that has happened in the universe. The *Yi*, a treatise explaining the symbolism, was first used for divination and for explaining both natural phenomena and human affairs, and later became a bridge between the teachings of opposing schools of philosophy in China.

All religions may be said to be products of the right side of the brain insofar as they stress faith rather than ratiocination in grasping the ultimate reality. Buddhism is an excellent example. The Buddhism which developed in China and moved into Japan and Korea, which is known philosophically as Mahāyāna, concluded that the Absolute is *śunyatā*, an emptiness which is affirmed, denied, both affirmed and denied, and neither affirmed nor denied. But what can this mean? It is nonsense to the intellect. A Western authority on

Buddhism advises, "Only systematic meditation can disclose its profundity. Emptiness is essentially an object of rapt contemplation, and inconclusive chatter about its being, or not being; 'nothingness' deserves only contempt. It would be a mistake to treat the views of the Mādhyamikas as though they were the result of philosophical reasoning, when in fact they derive from age-old meditational processes by which the intuition of the absolute is actually realized."[13]

Recent studies of Buddhist meditational trances demonstrate that the occurrence of conceptual thinking, such as the working out of a mathematical problem, will immediately remove the person from the state of trance.[14] This—in the language of the brain hemispheres—demonstrates that left-brain activity cancels right-brain activity.

The split brain analysis may be supported by appeal to the elaborate symbolism of hands in the Buddhist sculpture of Japan. Mochisuki Shinkyō in his book *Bukkyo daijiten* (Dictionary of Buddhism)[15] gives the following symbolism of the right and left hands:

Left Hand	*Right Hand*
Moon	Sun
Arresting the active mind	Observation
Contemplation	Wisdom
Blessedness	Knowledge
Principle	Reason
Inner	Outer

In interpreting this symbolism we must keep in mind that the right hand is controlled by the left side of the brain and is the symbol of observation, knowledge, and reason; the left hand is controlled by the right side of the brain, and is the symbol of contemplation. The right hand (left brain) is the "outer" and the left hand (right brain) is the "inner."

The symbolism of hands in Tantric Buddhism also conforms to the split brain analysis. The right hand (controlled by the left side of the brain) symbolizes intelligence, and the left hand (controlled by the right side of the brain) symbolizes meditation. The *Fudarakukaieki* states, "The left hand is Appeasement and is called Principle: this is the Matrix World. The right hand discerns diverse things and is called Knowledge: this is the Diamond World. . . The left hand is Concentration: the right hand is Wisdom."[16]

117

One could not find a clearer statement of the right side of the brain approach than this one from a contemporary Zen Buddhist: "By changing our ordinary way of viewing things, which is intellectual or dualistic, to a new way of thinking, which is intuitive or non-dualistic, we can see the world of the essential, and are then in the midst of what Mahāyāna and in particular Zen Buddhists mean by emancipation, or _nirvāṇa_."[17] The distinction D. T. Suzuki drew between _prajñā_-intuition and _vijñāna_-reasoning is precisely the distinction of the activities of the right-hemisphere and left-hemisphere of the brain.[18] Stewart W. Holmes and Chimyo Horioka were probably not thinking of the right hemisphere of the brain and the left hemisphere when they distinguished "casual thoughts" and "judgments" in the following advice regarding Zen meditation, but this is clearly a distinction of the two functions: "Put a pencil and paper beside you, to record thoughts that you will want to recall later; then you will free yourself from the effort of trying to remember them. Casual thoughts and reactions to the environment will pass through your mind [in the right hemisphere] and leave no effect. Judgments, beliefs, ideologies [formed by the left hemisphere] are not so innocuous; if possible, avoid them."[19] One of the tenets of Zen according to Holmes and Horioka is "Being a spectator while one is also a participant spoils one's performance." This is the meaning of the aphorism "When you eat, eat; when you sleep, sleep." To think and evaluate one's actions while acting is a disease. The haiku

> I sneezed:
> And lost sight
> Of the skylark

is a warning that to evaluate one's art while painting, one's golf while putting, one's diet while eating, one's worship while worshipping, or one's sexuality while making love may diminish both the quality and the enjoyment of the activity. A second haiku

> The long night:
> The sound of water
> Says my thought

is explained as follows: "The water does not comment on the night or on itself. Its sounds are part of the night."[20] The essence of Zen can

118

be expressed in the twin brain syndrome as paying enough attention to what one does to act but not enough attention to verbalize, cogitate, and evaluate.

Mahatma Gandhi was an excellent example of a right-brain person who remained right-brained despite a left-brain Western education. Nirad C. Chaudhuri maintains that Gandhi understood but never assimilated the intellectual approach of the West. He remained an "uneducated" mass man. "In the long history of their existence these masses have had many prophets to preach their ethos and voice their idealistic aspirations but none who so completely was their very own. Mahatma Gandhi remained theirs even after birth and education had done everything to bring about a separation. Neither his station in life nor his English education succeeded in making him understand the things of the intellect and civilization. He remained profoundly uneducated in the intellectual sense and lived in utter nakedness of spirit till his death."[21]

An interesting application of the split brain phenomenon in the West is the introduction of new techniques of instruction in art education. Betty Edwards in *Drawing on the Right Side of the Brain*[22] offers unusual suggestions for learning to draw; e.g., she has her students duplicate a drawing seen upside down as one means of quieting the left side of the brain.

Winston Churchill had no notion of the split brain, yet in his essay "Painting as a Pastime" he supported his hobby on the grounds that painting used a different part of his mind. "A man can wear out a particular part of his mind by continually using it and tiring it, just in the same way as he can wear out the elbows of his coat."[23] Churchill was on much firmer ground when he championed his hobby on the need for change. Reading, he said, is important, but it is "too nearly akin to the ordinary daily round of the brain-worker to give that element of change and contrast essential to real relief. To restore psychic equilibrium we should call into use those parts of the mind which direct both eye and hand."[24]

Thaddeus Kostrubala, an authority on jogging, has argued that repetitive long distance running, like repetitive mantras, wears out the left cortex and allows consciousness to take a peek at the functions of the right side of the brain.[25]

Psychologists are beginning to think of mental health as the integration of intuition and intellect. For example, Roberto Assagioli writes, "To speak more directly, and without metaphor, of the true relationship between intuition and intellect, intuition is the creative advance towards reality. Intellect [needs, first, to perform] the valuable and necessary function of interpreting, i.e., of translating, verbalizing in acceptable mental terms, the results of the intuition; second, to check its validity; and third, to coordinate and to include it into the body of already accepted knowledge. . . . A really fine and harmonious interplay between the two can work perfectly in a successive rhythm: intuitional insight, interpretation, further insight and its interpretation, and so on."[26]

The generalization that Western people overdevelop the left side of the brain and Eastern people overdevelop the right side needs further examination. In the volume *The Japanese Brain: Brain Function and East-West Culture* (1978), which has not yet been translated into English, the neurophysiologist Tadanobu Tsunado reports experiments performed in his laboratory at the Tokyo Medical and Dental University which seem to establish that Japanese minds function differently from Western minds, not because of inheritance but because of peculiarities of the Japanese language. The Japanese language and Polynesian languages are rich in vowels. A whole sentence may contain only vowel sounds, e.g., "*oe o ui, oi o ooi, ai o ou, aiueo.*" (A love-hungry man who worries about hunger hides his old age and chases love.)[27] In Western languages vowels are boxed in by consonants. The result is that minimal attention is required in order to hear words. But where the separating consonants are few, more attention is required. A case in point is the difficulty often experienced in listening to the words of a song as compared to hearing the words spoken. Another example is the problem many Western people have in hearing and pronouncing the native names of towns and cities in the Hawaiian Islands. The speakers of Japanese must pay careful attention to vowel sounds. This is done with the left hemisphere of the brain, the area of logical analysis and discrimination. The result is that Japanese-speaking persons also attend to nonverbal sounds, such as animal and natural sounds, more than do speakers of Western languages—even more than do persons of Japanese ancestry who have grown up in the West and have spoken only Western languages. Tsunado's studies of right-handed Westerners,

Koreans, Chinese, and Bengalis show that they process vowels on the right side of the brain. "Right-handed" because Tsunado finds that whereas right-handed people are strongly lateralized, left-handed people are less so. His experiments with brain-impaired people support his observation: "The Japanese and Polynesians also tend to depend on their left brains for processing nonverbal human utterances that express emotions—sounds such as laughing, crying, or sighing—along with natural sounds such as cricket chirps, cow calls, bird songs, and ocean waves. By contrast, those who speak European languages handle all these sounds in their right hemisphere."[28] This means that Japanese-speaking people are more consciously appreciative of the physical environment than are speakers of Western languages. Claps of thunder, babblings of brooks, chirps of insects, songs of birds, and calls of animals are for them the languages of nature. Even time is perceived differently.

The Hatter was in fact taking a Japanese attitude toward time when he rebuked Alice for referring to time as "it"—.

Alice sighed wearily. "I think you might do something better with the time," she said, "than wasting it in asking riddles that have no answers."

"If you knew Time as well as I do," said the Hatter, "you wouldn't talk about wasting *it*. It's *him*." (The Hatter, by the way, referred to Time with an uppercase T.)

Alice responded in a typical Western manner:

"I don't know what you mean."

"Of course you don't!" the Hatter said, tossing his head contemptuously. "I dare say you never even spoke to Time!"

"Perhaps not," Alice cautiously replied; "but I know I have to beat time when I learn music."

"Ah! That accounts for it," said the Hatter. "He won't stand beating."

"Beating time" is the Western attitude. Human existence is a race against time. "Beating the clock" is one of the clichés in basketball, football, soccer, and other timed sports. Every runner of distances from 100 meters to the marathon knows that his greatest competitor is the clock.

In Japan, according to Shin Ohara, the temporal remark heard

121

most often is *conouchi ni* ("in the course of time"). Time connotes the taking of turns. He writes, "In the Japanese system, we think of life as a cycle. We thus find a kind of analogy with natural cycles. In the annual cycle, nature is the subject, whereas in the social cycle, the senior is the subject. In both cases, one must patiently wait for something that will be given. The system of time presupposes the idea that all individuals are almost equal, and hence they can take turns one after another. . . . Japanese mothers seldom say 'no'; they say 'later.' "[29]

The traditional Japanese home is so related to the outside that while one is inside the house he has the illusion of being in the garden. The Japanese turn a simple act, like the drinking of a cup of tea, into a ceremony.

If it is the case that the Japanese process logical thought and emotional enjoyment on the same side of the brain, then they do not experience a dichotomy between thinking and feeling. We can infer that a Japanese person hears himself laugh—a phenomenon rarely experienced by a Western person. And if the Japanese have developed ways of living in harmonious interplay rather than destructive opposition in their natural and social environments, we in the West must observe carefully.

A curious evidence of the integration of right brain and left brain is found in the study of dreams of Western people; viz., dreams early in the sleeping period involve images which cannot be easily reported verbally, whereas dreams late in the sleeping period are easily transferred into verbal consciousness. One study reports that only 30% of dreams early in the night can be expressed verbally, but almost 100% of dreams late in the night can be expressed verbally. If my hypothesis that Orientals are right-brained and Occidentals are left-brained is true, then Western people go to sleep as Easterners and awake as Westerners![30]

The ideal congruity of reasoning and feeling has been adumbrated by a few Western poets. For example, Tennyson claimed in "In Memoriam" that

> A warmth within the breast would melt
> The freezing reason's colder part,
> And like a man in wrath the heart
> Stood up and answer'd, 'I have felt.'

122

And Yeats wrote in "A Prayer for Old Age"

> God guard me from those thoughts men think
> In the mind alone;
> He that sings a lasting song
> Thinks in a marrow-bone.

But perhaps the simplest statement of the ideal harmony of intellect and intuition is found in the collection of old Icelandic poems, the *Elder Edda*:

> The mind knows only
> What lies near the heart.

NOTES

1. See Michael S. Gazzaniga, "The Split Brain in Man" in *The Nature of Human Consciousness*. Ed. by Robert E. Ornstein. (New York: Viking, 1973), chap. 7.
2. *Bulletin of the Los Angeles Neurological Societies*, vol. 34, no. 3, July 1969.
3. This list is from *The Nature of Human Consciousness*, p. 111. Another excellent source of information about the split brain is Robert E. Ornstein, *The Psychology of Consciousness*. (New York: Viking, 1972), chap. 3. Charles Hampden-Turner in *Maps of the Mind*, (New York: Macmillan, 1981), p. 89, lists additional left-right hemisphere terms:

Left Hemisphere	Right Hemisphere	Creator of the Term
Scylla	Charybdis	(Homer)
Hubris	Nemesis	(Greek tragedy)
Yang	Yin	(*I Ching*)
Mind	Body	(Descartes)
Conscious	Unconscious	(Sigmund Freud)
Ego	Id	(Sigmund Freud)
Thinking	Feeling	(Carl Jung)
Sensation	Intuition	(Carl Jung)
Solitary	Solidary	(Albert Camus)
Positivist	Existential	(Rollo May)
Denial of Death	Death	(Ernest Becker)
Natural Religion	Fourfold Vision	(William Blake)
Commissar	Yogi	(Arthur Koestler)
Vertical thinking	Lateral thinking	(Edward de Bono)
I-it	I-thou	(Martin Buber)

123

Territory	Map	(Alfred Korzybski)
Object-level	Meta-level	(Bertrand Russell)
Surface structure	Deep structure	(Noam Chomsky)
Ego	Being	(Jonas Salk)
Positive	Mythic	(Claude Lévi-Strauss)

4. Pp. xi-xii.

5. Ornstein, *The Psychology of Consciousness*, pp. 61-62. See also Thomas R. Blakeslee, *The Right Brain.* (Garden City, New York: Anchor Press/ Doubleday, 1980), pp. 176-9.

6. Los Angeles: Tarcher, 1980, p. 79.

7. New York: Antheneum, 1965, pp. 5-6.

8. New York: Macmillan, 1946. See also "The Complementary Emphases of Eastern Intuitive and Western Scientific Philosophy" in *Philosophy— East and West*, ed. by Charles A. Moore. (Princeton: Princeton University Press, 1946), pp. 168-234.

9. *Philosophy—East and West*, p. 234.

10. *Ibid.*

11. Translated by Joseph Theman and Herbert Burke. (London: Sheed and Ward, 1957).

12. *Philosophy—East and West*, p. 205.

13. Edward Conze, *Buddhist Thought in India.* (Ann Arbor, Michigan: University of Michigan Press, 1967), pp. 243-4.

14. See Gay Gaer Luce and Julius Segal, *Sleep and Dreams.* (Panther, 1969), pp. 250-6. Also Yoel Hoffmann, *The Idea of Self—East and West.* (Calcutta: Firma KLM Private Limited, 1980), p. 104.

15. See E. Dale Saunders, *Mudrā. A Study of Symbolic Gestures in Japanese Buddhist Sculpture.* (New York: Pantheon, 1960), p. 33.

16. Saunders, *Mudrā*, pp. 30-1.

17. Sohaku Ogata, *Zen for the West.* (New York: Dial, 1959), p. 29.

18. See "Reason and Intuition in Buddhist Philosophy" in *Essays in East-West Philosophy*, pp. 17-48.

19. *Zen Art for Meditation.* (Rutland, Vermont: Charles E. Tuttle, 1973), p. 13.

20. *Ibid.*, p. 72.

21. *The Autobiography of an Unknown Indian.* (New York: Macmillan, 1951), p. 430.

22. Los Angeles: Tarcher, 1979.

23. *Painting as a Pastime*, p. 7.

24. *Ibid.*, pp. 12-13.

25. *The Joy of Running.* (New York: Simon and Schuster, 1976.) See also John

M. Silva III, "Psychological Aspects of Elite Long-Distance Running." *National Forum*, winter (1983), pp. 32-34, 37.

26. *Psychosynthesis: A Manual of Principles and Techniques*. (New York: Viking, 1971), p. 223.

27. The Gnostic Christians regarded vowel sounds to be more productive of religious ecstasy than consonant sounds. Hence one of their sacred chants was the following: "Zoxathazo a ōō ēē ōōō ēēē ōōōō ēē ōōōōōōōōōō ōōōōō uuuuuu ōōōōōōōōōō Zozazoth." (Elaine Pagels, *The Gnostic Gospels*. (New York: Random House, 1981), p. 164.)

28. Atuhiro Sibantani in a review of Tsunado's book in *Science 80*, December 1980, p. 25. Left handedness and right handedness were studied in 1861 by J. J. Bachofen in his book *Das Mutterrecht: Eine Untersuchung über die Gynaikokrative der alten Welt nach ihrer religiösen und rechlichen Natur. (Mother Right: An Investigation of the Religious and Juridical Character of Matriarchy in the Ancient World)*. He contended that the left hand is feminine, and he argued for *major honos laevarum partium* (greater honor of the left side). John Hick has recently suggested that left and right hemispheres of the brain may explain splits within the Christian community: "My own view is that the Christian mind will almost inevitably come to see the doctrine of the Incarnation, and the doctrine of the Trinity which grew out of it, in a new way, no longer as precise metaphysical truths but as imaginative constructions giving expression, in the religious and philosophical language of the ancient world, to the Christian's devotion to Jesus as the one who has made the heavenly Father real to him. Or at any rate, I would suggest that this is the kind of development which the more intellectual part of the Christian mind (appropriately, in the human brain, the left hemisphere!) is likely to undergo, whilst its more emotional other half perhaps continues to use the traditional language of Christian mythology without raising troublesome questions about its meaning." *God Has Many Names*. (London: Macmillan Press, 1980), p. 88.

29. Shin Ohara, "The Wheel of Time." *Science Digest*, November (1981), p. 73. Ohara does not refer to the Japanese obsession for having their railways run on time!

30. See Thomas R. Blakeslee, *The Right Brain*, pp. 31-36. Also David B. Cohen, "Changes in REM Dream Content during the Night: Implications for a Hypothesis About Changes in Cerebral Dominance across REM Periods." *Perceptual and Motor Skills*, vol. 44, (1977), pp. 1267-77. Also see Paul Bakan, "The Right Brain Is the Dreamer." *Psychology Today*, November (1976), pp. 66-68.

10. The Hindu Images of Man*

Maurice Friedman recommends the term "human image" be substituted for the term "human nature." "Human nature" connotes universality and permanence. "Human image" connotes individuality and change. "Nature" indicates status. "Image" indicates direction. "The nature of man" suggests what man is. "The image of man" suggests what man may become. Friedman has written, "The human image does not mean some fully formed, conscious model of what one *should* become—certainly not anything simply imposed on us by the culture or any mere conformity with society through identification with its goals. . . . The human image is our becoming in the truest sense of the word, that is, our becoming as a person and as a human being. In this becoming, what we call the 'is' is not a static given. It is a dynamic, constantly changing material that is continually being shaped and given form not merely by inner and outer conditioning but by the directions that one takes as a person."[1] Perhaps the plural—"images"—would be a better word. Certainly the shift from "human image" to "human images" is apropos when one is examining the Hindu view of man.

There is an opinion perpetuated by some Western scholars and by many Indians that Hinduism is of one piece, viz., a system of ideas, values, and practices stemming from the *Upaniṣads,* interpreted faithfully by Śaṅkara, and practiced paradigmatically by Vivekānanda, Tagore, Gandhi, and a few other well-known Indians. But a monolithic view of Hinduism will not bear close examination. Neither can we claim, as Gandhi did, that although there are two Hinduisms, one is false. Gandhi wrote in 1946, "There are two aspects of Hinduism . . . historical Hinduism with its untouchability, superstitious wor-

---

*The paper was read at the 17th World Congress of Philosophy, Montreal, Canada, August 21, 1983.

ship of sticks and stones, animal sacrifices and so on [the false Hinduism TO] . . . [and] the Hinduism of the *Gītā*, the *Upaniṣads*, and Patañjali's *Yoga Sūtra,* which is the acme of *ahiṃsā* . . . oneness of all creation, pure worship of . . . God." [the true Hinduism TO][2] Keshub Chunder Sen in 1861 described Brahmaism as "Human Catholic Religion."[3] I borrow his term to characterize Hinduism as "Human Catholicism," and I find three images of the human in Hinduism:

1. Man out of the world.
   The condition is known as *sannyāsa*.
   The person in the condition is a *sannyāsin*.
2. Man in the world.
   The condition is known as *nāgaraka*.
   The person in the condition is a *nāgarakin*.
3. Man on the way.
   The condition is known as *mārgāyata*.
   The person in the condition is a *mārgāyatin*.

The friends of Hinduism commonly stress the first image: the ideal human being is a celibate anchorite who has cloistered himself in a cave in the Himalayas where his disciples may come for his blessings. The enemies of Hinduism commonly stress the second image: the ideal human being is a cultured degenerate and dandy accomplished in the sixty-four arts and skills associated with the bedchamber. I am stressing the third image: the ideal human being is the one who is ever on the path of self-perfecting.

Some students of Hinduism puzzle over a bifurcation in Hindu culture; e.g., B.G. Gokhale noted in his book *Indian Thought through the Ages: A Study of Dominant Concepts* that "in the history of Indian thought there is always an interplay of two opposite trends running parallel to each other throughout the ages."[4] Gokhale cited as examples duty to others and self-seeking, sensuality and asceticism, and war and non-violence. He might have mentioned excess and deficiency, beauty and ugliness, and tradition and creativity. The lives of two twentieth-century Hindus are illustrative. Aurobindo shifted from political violence in Calcutta to quiet seclusion in Pondicherry. Vinoba Bhave desired to seek religious asylum in the Himalayas while a student at Banaras, later became the first disciple of Gandhi to engage in civil disobedience, and finally walked across India asking landowners to contribute portions of their holdings to the poor. The bifurcation of Hindu culture was also noted by Albert Schweitzer: "Hinduism possesses an astonishing capacity for overlooking or setting aside theoretical problems, because from time immemorial it has lived in a state of compromise between monotheism and polytheism, between pantheism and theism, between world and life negation and world and life affirmation and between supra-ethical and ethical ways of regarding things."[5] Akhileshwar Jha has written, "Contradictions are never resolved in Hinduism, they are permitted to stay side by side undisturbed by each other."[6]

Since about the fourth century A.D. the ideal human life of the Hindu has been divided into four chronological periods (āśramas):

1. *Brahmacarya.* The student years. The time of preparation.
2. *Gṛhasthya.* The family years. The time of caring for children and parents.
3. *Vānaprasthya.* The semi-retirement years. The time of training children to take over the family's responsibilities and of giving service to the community.
4. *Sannyāsa.* The full retirement years. The time of complete attention to one's salvation.

If liberation (*mokṣa*) is the *summum bonum* of human life, as Hinduism claims, then the fourth *āśrama* is the most important. Aurobindo has written, "When you have paid your debt to society, filled well and admirably your place in its life, helped its maintenance and continuity and taken from it your legitimate and desired satisfactions, there still remains the greatest thing of all. There is still your own self, the inner you, the soul which is a spiritual portion of the Infinite, one in its essence with the Eternal. This self, this soul in you you have to find, you are here for that."[7]

The *sannyāsa* image of man is constructed on the premise that the highest good for man is freedom as release from the agonies and frustrations of the human condition and freedom as opportunity to realize the potentialities of the human condition. The *sannyāsa āśrama* both follows and fulfills the student, householder, and citizen periods. It is a time of retirement, although not of idleness. The *sannyāsin* under the older interpretation renounced family ties, economic pursuits, and social activities in order to devote full attention to study, meditation, and prayer. In a sense it was a return to the life of the student. But, whereas the first student period was a preparation for marriage and career, the second was a preparation for the experience of death and what may lie beyond.

The *sannyāsa* image has changed through the years—and, I believe, is being radically changed in India today. Although one occasionally sees a wandering mendicant, their number appears to be diminishing. I recall a paper at the 1965 meeting of the Indian Philosophical Congress which raised the question "Does the old man need love?" A small group of older philosophers answered negatively. But a very vocal group of younger philosophers countered that according to modern psychology no one outgrows the need for love and affection. I gathered that the second group were of the opinion that the human life span cannot be neatly divided into four periods, and that the *āśramas* ought to be interpreted as four dimensions of human need: planning, nurturing, sharing, and harvesting.

Gandhi was right—there are two Hinduisms. But they are not the two he identified. The two differ as to the reality and value of man in the world. One regards the physical world and the individual human self as phenomenal and of little worth (*māyā*). The world lacks substantial reality. The self lacks attributable reality with respect to individuality. This is the Hinduism Albert Schweitzer in *Indian Thought and Its Development* described as "world and life negation." It can be located in the *Upaniṣads*, although those remarkable speculations contain a variety of views of man and his world. The other Hinduism regards the physical world and the individual human self as real and valuable (*sat*). This Hinduism is patent in the folk tales of the *Pañchatantra*, the rules for successful politics in the *Artha Śastra* of Kautilya (Post-Upaniṣadic), the hedonistic materialism of the Cārvāka system of philosophy (sixth century B.C. ff.), the moral maxims of the *Kural* of Tiruvaḷḷuvar (fifth century A.D.), and the enormous erotic literature of Tantrism. The former presents a *sannyāsa* image of man. The latter presents a *nāgaraka* image of man.

Sannyāsa is the way of defect. *Nāgaraka* is the way of excess. The *sannyāsin* is a forest dweller. The *nāgarakin* is a man about town. The *nāgarakin* celebrates the joy of existence in *līlā* (sport). *Līlā* in Hinduism is usually expressed in pluralities. Cosmic creation itself is the playful exuberance of the Demiurge. According to Aurobindo "a real diversity brings out the real Unity, shows it as it were in its utmost

129

capacity, reveals all that it can be and is in itself, delivers from its whiteness of hue the many tones of colour that are fused together there; Oneness finds itself infinitely in what seems to us to be a falling away from its oneness, but is really an inexhaustible display of unity."[8] The theme of the necessary sportive multiplication of a one appears frequently in Hindu theology; e.g., "One . . . fire blazeth forth in many shapes."[9] And in the *Mahābhārata* Agni, the fire god, celebrates his power to manifest himself: "Having, by ascetic power, multiplied myself, I am present in various forms."[10] Śiva has 108 classical dance poses. One hall in the Naṭarāja temple at Chidambaram has 984 pillars. Kṛṣṇa had 16,008 wives. The number of Vedic gods was said to be 330,000,000. In the *Rāmāyaṇa* Rāvana's forces included 150,000,000 elephants and 300,000,000 horses. These huge numbers are not the exaggeration of childish minds but an expression of delight in plurality and diversity.

The life of the *nāgarakin* is fully prescribed. He cleans his teeth and scrapes his tongue daily, anoints his body every third day, shaves his beard every fourth day, cuts his finger nails every fifth day, shaves his entire body every tenth day, has an enema every twelfth day, takes a laxative every thirtieth day, and has a phlebotomy every six months. All these are done in order that hedonic satisfactions, expecially the sexual ones, be intense. The *Kāma Sūtra* lists sixty-four arts auxillary to the joys of love, ten kinds of kisses, eight kinds of scratchings, eight kinds of bitings, twelve non-coital forms of embrace, and eighty-four coital positions. (One commentator—Masodhra—says the number is 729!) But the *nāgarakin* is not a roué. He and his mistress are supposed to conversant in 528 subject matters.

The *nāgaraka* image of man is most clearly depicted in Tantric literature. My own experience in India supports the claim of Bharati Agehananda that he has never found a living Hindu who stands by the Tantric tradition.[11] In 1968 after delivering a public lecture on Tantrism I was verbally attacked by a Bengali Brahmin. He admitted there were erotic images in some temples and that *liṅga* worship was common, but he informed me that modern Hindus do not mix religion and sex—and he wished that I as a Westerner would avoid such topics. A few from the audience came to me later to express another opinion—but they did not speak out in public.

Although Cārvāka is not an orthodox *darśana* (system of thought), it was not silenced so soon or so completely as some historians of Indian philosophy claim. For example, the _Sarvasiddhāntasaṁgraha_, a fourteenth century A.D. writing, states, "There is no world other than this; there is no heaven and no hell. . . . The enjoyment of heaven lies in eating delicious food, keeping company of young women, using fine clothes, perfumes, garlands, and sandal paste. The pain of hell lies in the troubles that arise from enemies, weapons, diseases; while liberation is death which is the cessation of life-breath. . . . Chastity and other such ordinances are laid down by clever weaklings."[12]

The _Artha Śāstra_ contains practical advice on the art of ruling. Officers should be rotated, lest they become entrenched in power. Enemy kingdoms are to be weakened by fomenting disturbances within them. Personal enemies are to be tortured, blinded, exposed to contagious diseases, and murdered. Likewise in the _Mahābhārata_ the king is advised in taxation to "act like the leech drawing blood. . . . A little by little should be taken. . . . Acting with care and mildness the king should at last put the reins on the people."[13]

The _Pañchatantra_ is a collection of folk stories which have been current among the people of the subcontinent of Asia for at least 5000 years. Arthur Ryder, who has translated them, describes the tales as a textbook of _nīti_, i.e., the wise conduct of life.[14] The _Pañchatantra_ is a program for the attainment of success, profit, and pleasure. Fragments of three poems suggest the mood of the work:

> A fangless snake, an elephant
> Without an ichor-store;
> A man who lacks a cash account—
> Are names and nothing more.[15]

> The wealthy, though of meanest birth,
> Are much respected on the earth:
> The poor whose lineage is prized
> Like clearest moonlight, are despised.[16]

> Money gets you anything,
> Gets it in a flash:
> Therefore let the prudent get
> Cash, cash, cash.[17]

131

An Englishman who had lived in India thirty years told me that he never understood the Indian character until he read the *Pañchatantra*.

I wish now to return to Mahatma Gandhi. I perceive him as a complex man who masqueraded as a simple man. He was one in whom the images of *sannyāsa* and *nāgaraka* were never integrated. But maybe I do him injustice. T. H. Mahadevan sees him differently: "Here I think is the core of the Gandhi image—of a man endlessly, tirelessly in search of truth. Nandlal Bose, in that famous linocut, immortalized the walking Gandhi, the eternal pilgrim with the staff in hand and the forward gait, moving endlessly on, never looking back. But Gandhi was more than a pilgrim; he was an indefatigable searcher for truth. . . . With some pardonable exaggeration, I would say that the Indian mind's search for truth, which we find so intensely portrayed in Gandhi, began millennia ago in the *Rig Veda*: 'What thing I truly am, I know not clearly. Mysterious, fettered in my mind, I wander.' It is a search which has a beginning but no end."[18] If this is a correct assessment, then Gandhi was a *mārgāyatin*—one on the way, one in whom the four *āśramas* appeared simultaneously rather than seriatim, one who was a *sannyāsa-nāgarkin* or a *nāgarka-sannyāsin*. There are passages in the writings of Gandhi which express this image; e.g., "Let us be sure of our ideal. We shall ever fail to realize it, but shall never cease to strive for it."[19] "Satisfaction lies in the effort, not in the attainment. Full effort is full victory."[20]

The *mārgāyata* image of man has a long tradition in Hinduism. We read from the *Aitareya Āraṇyaka*, "Whatever man reaches he desires to go beyond it."[21] The life of dynamic perfecting has been associated in the last century particularly with the lives of Vivekananda and Tagore. For example, Vivekananda said, "Man is to become divine, realizing the divine more and more from day to day in an endless progress."[22] And according to Rabindranath Tagore, "Man is not complete; he is yet to be. In what he *is* he is small, and if we could conceive him stopping there for eternity we should have an idea of the most awful hell that man can imagine. In his *to be* he is infinite, there is his heaven, his deliverence. His *is* is occupied every moment with what it can get and have done with; his *to be* is hungering for something which is more than can be got, which he never can lose because he never has possessed."[23]

The harmonized polarity of *sannyāsa* and *nāgaraka*, of saintliness and hedonism, of spirit and matter is not yet accomplished in Hindu culture—or are we to conclude that instability is essential to the *mārgāyata* image? For example, two well-qualified Indian intellectuals wrote the following about Indian art and spirituality:

"The essential quality of Indian art is its pre-occupation with things of the spirit."[24] (Vasudeva S. Agrawala)
"The claim . . . made by both the admirers and the detractors of Indian culture that the people here were highly religious, and therefore exclusively otherworldly, is both spurious and unreasonable. . . . The truth is that Hinduism as a religion offers much larger scope for full- blooded earthly life than does the religion of Christ. All the varieties of fine arts, including dance and painting, formed an essential part of popular Hinduism."[25] (N.K. Devaraja)

Rāmānuja in his interpretation of the Upaniṣadic pronouncement *tat tvam asi* said that *tat* refers to Brahman in the causal state (*kāranāvasthā*), and that *tvam* refers to Brahman in the effected state (*kāryāvasthā*). Inasmuch as man-the-*Ātman* shares in these states, we can affirm that man is both man-qua-cause and man-qua-effect. Man is *natura naturans* (nature creating) and *natura naturata* (nature created). Creation-discovery is man's true image. In yoga this is known as *kaivalya* (restoration). But "restoration" does not have the correct connotation. Fixity or return to an original perfection from which man has fallen does not belong in the *mārgāyata* view of man. Man is to live a full (*pūrṇa*) life, and that fullness is forward, not backward. We err if we relate *pūrṇa* with the Latin *Perfectum*. Betty Heinmann expressed this excellently: "*Perfectum* must be translated as 'done through and through,' till the very final end of its possibilities is reached. This ideal of the final goal of Perfection is a Western postulate, not an Indian one. The West thinks on results, believes in facts which ultimately can be reached and fulfilled. . . . The Indian mind, on the other hand, rejoices in dynamic changes and divergent possibilities as a congenial expression of divine productivity. . . . The Western ideal rests in perfection, the fulfilment of a distinct aim which can be accomplished by limitation and selection only. The end, the ideal, is static and changeless in its perfected individuality. By contrast, the Indian is never satisfied with any static end."[26]

If *mārgāyata* is the fundamental image of man in Hinduism, what is the role of *sannyāsa and nāgaraka?* Must the way be a balance between defect and excess? Must the way of self-perfecting (*ātmansiddha*) go through a stage of *nāgaraka* and *sannyāsa?* Gandhi reported that he went through a period of smoking, meat-eating, wearing of fancy Western clothes, and excessive sexual congress before he became a non-smoker, extreme vegetarian, wearer of the loin cloth, and a practitioner of continence. Does it make sense to argue that the assassin's bullet stopped his pilgrimage at the *sannyāsa* level? He had gone through a *nāgaraka* stage. He had reached the sannyāsa stage. He stated often that he planned to live 110 years. Was he moving to a human condition in which *sannyāsa* and *nāgaraka* would have been integrated?

Perhaps there is another approach to an understanding of the three images of man in Hinduism, and this has to do with the Indian way of thinking. Art is one of the best methods for perceiving this fact. As Edith Hamilton has said, "A Hindoo temple is a conglomeration of adornment. The lines of the building are completely hidden by the decorations. Sculptured figures and ornaments crowd its surface, stand out from it in thick masses, break it up into a bewildering series of irregular tiers. It is not a unity but a collection, rich, confused. . . . The Greek temple is the perfect expression of the pure intellect illuminated by the spirit. No other great buildings anywhere approach its simplicity."[27] The Greek way of thinking was restrained, balanced, straightforward, circumscribed. The Greek term for this was *sōphrōn*. The ideal was expressed in such maxims as "Think mortal thoughts," "Let no man soar to the heavens nor try to wed Aphrodite," (Alcman) and "Be midway in the state." (Phocylides) But *sōphrōn* for the Indian is a balance between excess and defect. The *mārgāyata* is the man whose *mārga* is an existential transcendence of *nāgaraka* and *sannyāsa*. Integration in Hinduism is an integration of extremes. In Hegelian terminology—the synthesis (*mārgāyata*) is experienced only in and through the thesis (*nāgaraka*) and the antithesis (*sannyāsa*).

To be human is to be in process of becoming human. Man's being is his becoming. He is the not yet. He is the one on the way. Being on the way is his nature. Man is the *mārgāyatin*. As Julian Huxley and Pierre Teilhard de Chardin said, unconscious evolution (i.e., natural selection) has brought man to his present state. His further evolution is in his hands. Conscious evolution or annihilation are the only two possibilities. The price of self-awareness is plan or perish. Man searches to understand himself in order to become himself. What man is is the search for man. His being is such that were he to cease the quest for self-identity he would cease to be human. As Aristotle might say, he would then be either a beast, i.e., one that does not engage in the quest, or a god, i.e., one that does not need to engage in the quest. Man's being is the meaningful direction of his becoming. Man's highest good is an ever-renewed commitment to human growth.

On May 7, 1941, the day of his eightieth birthday and exactly three months before his death, Rabindranath Tagore delivered an address entitled "Crisis in Civilization." The outbreak of war in Europe had saddened him. He said, "I had at one time believed that the springs of civilization would issue out of the heart of Europe. But today when I am about to quit the world that faith has gone bankrupt altogether. . . . And yet I shall not commit the grievous sin of losing faith in Man."[28] This faith he had expressed in an earlier poem:

> There on the crest of the hill
>   stands the Man of Faith among the snow-white
>   silence.
> He scans the sky for some signal of light,
> and when the clouds thicken and the nightbirds
>   scream as they fly,
> he cries, "Brothers, despair not, for Man is great.[29]

NOTES

1. "Philosophical Anthropology and Psychotherapy." *Philosophy in Context*, vol. 12, (1982), p. 14. The italics are mine. See also Maurice Friedman, *Problematic Rebel, To Deny Our Nothingness*, and *The Hidden Human Image*.
2. *Harijan*, December 8, 1946.
3. See Prosanto Kumar Sen, *Biography of a New Faith*. (Calcutta: Thacker, Spink and Co., vol. I, 1950), p. 250.
4. Bombay: Asia Publishing House, 1961, p. 174.
5. *Indian Thought and Its Development*. (Boston: Beacon, 1957), pp. 223-4.

6. *The Imprisoned Mind.* (New Delhi: Ambika, 1980), p. 11.
7. *The Foundations of Indian Culture.* (New York: The Sri Aurobindo Library, The Greystone Press, 1953), p. 130.
8. *The Life Divine.* (New York: The Sri Aurobindo Library, The Greystone Press, 1949), p. 308.
9. *Mahābhārata, Vana Parva,* Section 134. Pratap Chandra Roy translation. (Calcutta: Oriental Publishing Co., n.d.), vol. 3, p. 285.
10. *Ibid., Adi Parva,* Section 7. *Ibid.,* vol. 1, p. 53.
11. *The Tantric Tradition.* (London: Rider and Co., 1965), p. 11.
12. *A Source Book in Indian Philosophy,* ed. by Sarvepalli Radhakrishnan and Charles A. Moore. (Princeton: Princeton University Press, 1958), p. 235.
13. *Santi Parva,* Section 88.
14. *The Pañchatantra.* Trans. by Arthur W. Ryder. (Bombay: Jaico Publishing House, 1949), p. 4.
15. *Ibid.,* pp. 207-8.
16. *Ibid.,* p. 219.
17. *Ibid.,* p. 374.
18. "An Approach to the Study of Gandhi" in *Quest for Gandhi,* ed. by G. Ramachandran and T. K. Mahadevan. (Bombay: Bharatiya Vidya Bhavan, 1970), pp. 261-2.
19. *Speeches and Writings.* (Madras: G.A. Natesan and Co., 1918), p. 363.
20. *Selections from Gandhi,* ed. by Nirmal Kumar Bose. (Ahmedabad: Navajivan Publishing House, 1948), p. 30.
21. 2. 1. 3.
22. *The Complete Works of Swami Vivekananda.* 11th ed. (Calcutta: Advaita Ashram, 1962), vol. 1, p. 332.
23. *Sādhanā.* (New York: Macmillan Co., 1914), p. 153.
24. Vasudeva S. Agrawala, *The Heritage of Indian Art.* (New Delhi: Ministry of Information and Broadcasting, Government of India, 1964), p. 7.
25. N.K. Devaraja, *The Mind and Spirit of India.* (Delhi: Motilal Banarsidass, 1967), pp. 2-3.
26. *Facets of Indian Thought.* (New York: Schocken Books, 1964), pp. 142-3.
27. *The Greek Way.* (New York: *Time* Incorporated, 1963), p. 50.
28. *Faith of a Poet: Selections from Rabindranath Tagore,* ed. by Sisirkumar Ghose. (Bombay; Bharatiya Vidya Bhavan, 1964), p. 55.
29. *The Vishvabharati Quarterly,* vol. 26, nos. 3 and 4, p. 48.

11. Time and Polarity in Hinduism

There is an old Hindu story of a man who fell into an elephant trap in the forest. It was a deep hole covered with fragile brush and grass. The unfortunate man caught hold of a vine which temporarily kept him from falling to the bottom of the trap. He looked down and saw a hungry lion in the trap waiting for him to fall. He looked up and saw two mice gnawing the vine. At that moment a few drops of honey fell into his mouth. As he tasted the sweet honey he exclaimed, "How good is life to furnish us with such sweetness." This is man's life, says the storyteller. We are headed for destruction, and yet we salvage optimism from impending doom.

Optimism sometimes assumes curious forms. Optimism in politicians often appears as what I call "Callipygianism." Historians of Greek sculpture refer to a much admired statue of Venus as "The Callipygian Venus." The term *callipygian* is formed from the word *kallos* (beautiful) and the word *pugē* (buttocks). The statue is so named because the sculptor did an exceptionally fine job on that portion of Venus' anatomy. The optimism which comes from those in political office is callipygian in that it is often couched in beautiful "buts." "Inflation increases, *but* the administration believes it is leveling off." "Unemployment rose two points last month, *but* that was less than was anticipated." "The cost of food was more last week, *but* the rate of increase is less than it has been for five months." In other words, things are bad; *but* take heart—they are getting worse more slowly!

I do not object to optimism. I submit that without some form of optimism the people perish. But I have doubts about some of the kinds of optimism offered to us. I do not respond positively when a millenarian Christian tells me to rejoice since things are going so badly that surely the second coming is near, or when a Hindu says that evil is a clear sign for rejoicing, as that means we are well into the

137

Kali Age. I have profited from reading J. Peter Vajk's *Doomsday Has Been Cancelled*. It removes some of the impact of Alvin Toffler's *Future Shock*. But I am not convinced that becoming "solar citizens," as Vajk recommends, will solve the problems of earthlings.

The belief in progress has been a ruling idea—if not *the* ruling idea—in Western thought for the past two centuries. We must not suppose that optimism and progress have always been dominant in Western thought. Pessimism was common among the Greeks and Romans. Horace, for example, wrote that "our parents' generation, inferior to that of our grandparents, brought forth ourselves who are more worthless still and are destined to have children yet more corrupt."[1] Somervell has abridged this to:

> Degenerate sires' degenerate seed,
> We'll soon beget a fourth-rate breed.

The first event in this century which challenged the belief in continuous and uniform progress was World War I. An economic depression, the civil rights movement, the population explosion, food shortages, the energy crisis, and additional military conflicts have made the belief more difficult. When politicians face honestly some of the social problems of our day, their therapy is usually antiquated. Gerard O'Neill of the Department of Physics at Princeton University contends that the human race has tried political solutions for 10,000 years, and that it is time to try another solution. O'Neill proposes that we begin building space capsules in order that human beings may in the future live out their lives in space between the earth and the moon. He speculates that eventually the space people will discover the earth, will colonize it, and will seed a new Renaissance. I offer a more modest proposal—one that is neither political nor physical. I—like Epicurus and Lucretius—propose that we simplify our lives. Bergson warned early in this century that we are moving in the direction of greater luxury and greater complexity, and that we are in danger of being converted into sybaritic ants. My proposal is that we begin the simplification process by adapting to our culture two insights from Hinduism: (1) the concept of nonlinear time, and (2) the concepts of nondestructive dualisms.

Most students of recent Western history agree that the West is

138

seriously, and perhaps fatally, ill. I wish to remind you what a few of these students have said.

Henry Adams wrote in 1904 that Western civilization is coming to an early terminus. He said there are four ages of Western history. The first is the Age of Religious Thought. It lasted 90,000 years, coming to an end in 1600. The second is the Mechanical Age, a period of 300 years, which ended in 1900. The third is the Electrical Age, which Adams said would last eighteen years. And the final is the Ethereal Age, which would last four years. Adams could see no future beyond 1922. We shall accelerate to oblivion, he said.

Another social prophet of the Western world, Oswald Spengler, was a German teacher of mathematics, who published after World War I a book entitled *The Decline of the West*. He believed that all civilizations go through four stages which he called "the four seasons." The West is now in the winter season. This stage is marked by the rise of large cities, dictatorship of money, slavery to machines, intellectual skepticism, and war. Spengler said the decline of the West is inevitable.

Pitirim Sorokin, a Russian immigrant who rose to become chairman of the Department of Sociology at Harvard University, argues in his *Cultural and Social Dynamics*, that we in the West are passing from the Sensate type of culture in which reality and value are measured in terms of sensory experiences into an Ideational type of culture in which religious and ascetic values are emphasized. But in the passage our whole Sensate culture will collapse. The transition cannot be prevented; we can only retard it or make it less violent. He wrote in 1957, "It is high time to realize that this is not one of the ordinary crises which happen almost every decade, but one of the greatest transitions in human history." We must prepare ourselves, says Sorokin, for a complete change of contemporary mentality and a fundamental transformation of our system of values.

Two other Western interpreters of history have been more appealing. One of these is Arnold Toynbee who said that Western society is losing its vitality and creative power because of our militarism, our idolatry of institutions, and our worship of the machine. He held that a profound moral and spiritual transformation may arrest the decline, and he discussed the possibility of a universal religion. The other is Albert Schweitzer, who rooted our Western illness in our lack

139

of regard for reasoning, our decay in moral convictions, our narrow specializations, and our prejudices of race and nation. He offered a healing through an all-encompassing ethical attitude he called "reverence for life."

Another observer of Western civilization has been far less optimistic. He is Lewis Mumford. In 1946 when most Americans were rejoicing in the end of World War II and in high hopes for the United Nations, Mumford wrote with the overtones of a Jeremiah: "If the dismantling of every factory, if the extirpation of every item of scientific knowledge that has been accumulated since 1600, were the price for mankind's continuance, we must be ready to pay that terrible price."

Other analysts of Western history could be cited—Hegel, Marx, Vico, Comte, Croce, Bury, Collingwood, Becker, Niebuhr, Berdyaev, and others—but these suffice to indicate that Western civilization is in no ordinary crisis. Adams and Spengler advise resignation; Sorokin thinks we can delay the collapse; Toynbee, Schweitzer, and Mumford hold faint hopes for a remedy. When we read these authors today, we feel a certain sense of quaintness. From the point of view of 1986 all of them seem to contain a Wilkins Micawber syndrome. Even in their pessimism they seem to be "waiting for something to turn up." Today we are faced with the same problems, but we feel a new urgency. Abraham J. Hershel puts it correctly when he says, "New in this age is an unparalleled awareness of the terrifying seriousness of the human situation. Questions we seriously ask today would have seemed utterly absurd twenty years ago, such as, for example: Are we the last generation? Is this the very last hour for Western civilization?"[2] Hershel epitomizes the malaise which has overtaken us in the West when he says, "He who would write a book in the praise of man would be regarded as a half-wit or a liar."[3] There are books which take a different view, to be sure. Vajk's _Doomsday Has Been Cancelled_ is such a book. He is certainly correct in his statement, "We are the future Makers." My argument is that the "we" must include Eastern as well as Western peoples.

The notion that the Western world can heal itself, that we can find within our own traditions the resources we need, may be part of the problem. The expectation that with a few more laws, a new arrangement of administrative plumbing, more workshops, more task forces, more committees, and more conferences we can solve our problem, is sophomoric. Gabriel Marcel has said that "the crisis which Western man is undergoing is a metaphysical one," and he adds, "There is probably no more dangerous illusion than that of imagining that some readjustment of social or institutional conditions could suffice of itself to appease a contemporary sense of disquiet which rises, in fact, from the very depth of man's being." Most politicians and church leaders are guilty of perpetuating this dangerous illusion. We must look deeper for the cause of our illness. We must look wider for the cure.

The impasse which our modern social prophets have predicted and we have reached, is one in which part of the problem is the notion that the solution lies within the Western tradition. Frederick Platt in an article in *Harpers*, November 1975, demonstrates the shallowness of some students of our illness when he seriously argues that decline in the study of Latin is the cause and that a return to Latin is the remedy! He writes, "The world is always in a mess, but sometimes in a worse mess than usual. The present is obviously one of those times, and there can be but one cause: the decline of Latin." Rest assured— I am not going to argue that learning Sanskrit is our panacea. Nor am I going to recommend that we join any Eastern cult. Rather I contend that we Western people must examine the assumptions of our culture. Is the value-free pursuit of truth any longer a virtue? Has the law of noncontradiction any priority? Should human lives always be preserved? When can civil laws be rightfully broken? What claims can a nation justly make on its citizens? What relevance have religious traditions? The crisis of Western civilization has come to pass under the aegis of our Western assumptions. I suggest we need to look beyond the West for therapy. I shall only hint at the possibility by appealing to the conceptions of time and polarity in Hindu culture.

The language and images we use for time reveal our Western assumptions. As Kant says, we represent the time sequence by a line progressing to infinity. We speak of time as an arrow shooting into the unknown. Time moves. We image it as destructive. It is the ravager which uses us and discards us. Time lays us low, cuts us down, destroys us. At the end of each year we picture time as an old man with a scythe. The old man is pushed aside by a baby who is the

141

new year with all its promises of good things to come. But the baby becomes the destructive old man with the scythe. However, there is another view of time in the West. This is the view that time is opportunity. The future is open-ended. All things are possible. The idea of progress is linked with the conception of time as filled with possibilities. Future events are sometimes emergent events. Not all that takes place is determined by the past. But the problem is that we Western people hold psychoneurotically to both views. Our view of time is destructive-opportunity or opportunitive-destruction.

In modern India time is not taken very seriously. V. S. Naipaul in *India: A Wounded Civilization* writes, "India, Hindu India, is eternal; conquests and defilements are but instants in time."[4] He reports that the Indian novelist R. K. Narayan said to him in London in 1961, "India is eternal."[5] Naipaul describes this as a "sentimental conviction."[6] He writes, "Out of a superficial reading of the past, then, out of the sentimental conviction that India is eternal and forever revives, there comes not a fear of further defeat and destruction, but an indifference to it. India will somehow look after itself; the individual is freed of all responsibility."[7] The 1975 Emergency was the crisis "of a wounded civilization that has at last become aware of its inadequacies and is without the intellectual means to move ahead."[8] Naipaul, an Indian who has lived entirely outside India, writes, "India remains so little known to Indians."[9] His reason for this claim is that "history . . . social inquiry, and the habits of analysis . . . are too far outside the Indian tradition."[10] India, argues Naipaul, must see its past—and must see it as *dead*; if not, the past will kill.[11]

In Hinduism cosmical time is conceived in such large numbers as to be psychologically meaningless. Calendar time was borrowed from the Greeks. While a wristwatch is a status symbol in India, one soon learns that it does not insure punctuality. A business meeting scheduled for 10:00 in the morning will get under way a few minutes before 11:00. I have spent as much as two hours in cashing a check in a bank in India.

Hindus believe that time moves in cycles rather than in a straight line. Time, whether conceived in terms of epochs or years or days, is believed to have two wings known as "day" and "night" and they are separated by two intermediate periods known as "dawn" and "twilight." In Hinduism time is primarily a psychological measurement. Objective time is relatively unimportant. The "length" of a period of time is how long it feels. To speak of "geological time" or of "the history of the universe" is to speak anthropomorphically. The length of time depends upon the state of development of the experiencer. The more advanced a person is in his total human development the less is his awareness of temporality. A *sannyāsin* is said to transcend time consciousness. But to be unconcerned about the passage of time does not mean to hold time to have no value. Indeed, while the Hindu seems to be unaware of the pressure of time, he may value it more than we do in the West. For example, Alan Watts tells of a friend who noticed that certain parts of a tea plantation near Darjeeling were in very bad shape. Upon inquiring, he found that the manager of the plantation had recently doubled the hourly wage. The result was that the workers appeared for only half the number of hours per week they had formerly worked. The workers, finding they could support themselves and their families by working half as long under the new salary scale, worked at the plantation only halftime so they would have more time for doing what they enjoyed more than picking tea. They valued free time more than extra money. I am reminded of the lines of W. H. Davies in his poem entitled "Leisure."

> What is life, if full of care
> We have no time to stand and stare?

The Hindu view challenges our view of progress which is linked with our linear view of time. For us to move in time is to develop, to advance, to improve. Spencer's theory of evolution became the basis for a theory of progress. Thomas Huxley speculated about "a great year" with its upward and downward routes. But few listened to him. In Hinduism evolution is balanced with involution. A movement from the one to the many is countered by a movement from the many to the one. The universe is thought to go through a long period of construction and then a long period of destruction. Mythologically these periods are described as Śiva resting and Śiva dancing, or as Viṣṇu asleep and Viṣṇu awake. Day becomes night, and night becomes day. Death follows life, and life follows death. Rebirth is the death of death. The absoluteness and the finality which we feel about the passage of time becomes in India harmony and rhythm. Old age is not the prelude to annihilation but the fulfillment of an incarnation and the door to further development. The essence of the doctrine of reincarnation is not that we return in another form, but that our perfecting does not end with what we call death. Whereas conservatives in the West locate values in the past and liberals locate values in the future, Hindus ask, "Why all the fuss about past and future? What does time have to do with goodness, beauty, and truth?"

Is it possible for Western people to alter their conception of time? Let me suggest that alterations are already taking place. First, we are aware of the strangeness of referring to two sorts of time: subjective and objective, the time we feel and the time that is. Is time ever a thing that is? Does the universe keep time? Is there any sense in speaking of geological time or astronomical time? Or is objective time merely one of the tricks man tries to play on the universe? Secondly, we can note that Leibniz in his theory of pre-established harmony and Bergson in his theory of durée presented very non-Western theories of time. For Leibniz the present exists timelessly in the future, and for Bergson the present is rolled up in the past. William James spoke of "the camel's hump of the present" which shades off into the past in the form of memory and into the future in the form of expectation. Is this what the Psalmist meant when he said that for God a day is as a thousand years and a thousand years is as a day? Man is the time-binding animal. We ought not to be slaves to time.

A third evidence of new thinking about time comes from modern astronomy. We are hearing about "black holes" in space. These are stars in a state of high compression. More recently astronomers are also speaking of "white holes," that is, stars in a state of a new beginning. Some astronomers speculate that the universe itself may go through an expanding process and a contracting process with a state between known as the "event horizon." This, if I am not mistaken, is very much like what R. D. Tolman of the California Institute of Technology was saying shortly after Einstein formulated the theory of an expanding universe. George Gamow openly rejects a linear view of time. He theorizes a creation of the universe in terms of a singular state some five billion years ago in which the galaxies were packed so closely as to provide the thermonuclear conditions for the synthesis of the elements—and he admits the possibility of antecedent states of the universe perhaps of a cyclic nature. E. T. Whittaker argues that there was an epoch about 10^9 or 10^{10} years ago on the other side of which the cosmos may have existed in some form totally unlike anything known to us. W. de Sitter has written that "the solution of the field-equations of the theory of relativity shows that there is in the universe a tendency to change its scale, which at the present time results in an expansion, but may perhaps at other times become, or have been, a shrinking." H. Bondi, T. Gold, and Fred Hoyle argue for a steady-state condition of the expanding universe— a theory known also as continous creation—in which matter is being created in all epochs and throughout space at a statistically uniform rate, a creation which is sufficient to compensate for the continuing expansions of the universe, and hence an overall constant density. This might be described as a situation in which the "beginning" of the universe is always *now*!

In the fourth place we must note that there have been a few who have interpreted Western civilization cyclically. The pattern has been one of eschatology and rebirth. Seneca is a classic example. He wrote, "A single day will see the burial of all mankind. All that the long forbearance of fortune has produced, all that is beautiful, great thrones, great nations—all will descend into the one abyss, will be overthrown in one hour. . . . When the destruction of the human race is consummated . . . the ancient order of things will be recalled. Every living creature will be created fresh. The earth will receive a new man ignorant of sin, born under happier stars. But they, too, will retain their innocence only while they are new. Vice quickly creeps in."[12] The Greek and Roman cyclical views of time were circular. Socrates will again have to marry Xanthippe and drink the hemlock. "What has happened will happen again, and what has been done will be done again, and there is nothing new under the sun."[13] Origen likewise thought that a cyclical view of time meant depressing repetition: "this must mean that Adam and Eve will again do what they did before, there will again be the same flood, the same Moses will once more lead a people numbering 600,000 out of Egypt, Judas also will twice betray his Lord, Saul will a second time keep the clothes of those who stone Stephen, and we must say that all that has been done in this life is destined to be done again."[14]

But the Hindu time cycle is a helix. Viṣṇu is incarnated at the end of every cosmic cycle, but each incarnation involves a genuine novel-

145

ty. Each incarnation is unique. Each is different from the other incarnations. It is this difference in sameness which allows for a conception of progress without the obsession over progress which is characteristic of modern Western civilization.

We in the West are constantly thinking in terms of opposites: male and female, youth and age, individual and society, man and God, freedom and law, science and religion, right and wrong. Not so among the Hindus. They postulate juxtaposition and identity. The two which we see as the dichotomy of opposites they see as the identity of polarities. For example, to say "I am God" is the ultimate blasphemy in the West; but in India the existential discovery *Tat tvam asi* (That you are) is the highest and noblest goal of the human pilgrimage. The Western conflict of generations is among Hindus a harmony of differences. Young people enjoy their youth and look forward to becoming adults like their parents. A home without three generations is less than a home. Grandchild and grandparent belong. Each station in life has its duties and its privileges. When each does what the role requires, the home, the school, the city, and the nation come to be; or conversely, one fulfills one's role as wife, husband, student, teacher, citizen, ruler in the doing of what the station requires. One becomes one's self, not in destroying another or in defeating another, but in the strange pattern of differing enough to complement the other. As the Chinese might say, the Tao becomes Tao in the Yin-ing of the Yang and in the Yang-ing of the Yin. Jung calls them *Animus* and *Anima*.

The term *polarity*, of course, comes from the word *pole* and is related to words like *end, extremity, opposite, terminal point,* and *goal.* Polarity is a form of dualism, or, to state this conversely, there are two forms of dualism, the polar and the nonpolar. In a nonpolar dualism the two fundamental realities are separate, independent, unique, and noncontiguous. The problem of establishing causal relations between nonpolar realities in a dualistic system leads to that peculiar form of agnosticism known as interactionism or to that strange noncausal relationship known as parallelism or to some equally unsatisfactory explanatory technique. But in polar dualism the two fundamental realities are both joined and disjoined. Polar entities are harmonious discords or contrasting concords. They are the extremities of a single whole. Whereas a void sunders nonpolar dual

146

entities, the "space" between polar dual entities is filled. Poles are the necessary opposites of a single reality. Conflict *and* reconciliation are inherent in polarity. Polar duals exhibit repulsion and attraction, rejection and acceptance, discord and harmony, strife and love, confrontation and mutualism.

Nonpolar duality is illustrated in the Western pattern of good and evil. An unbridgeable gulf separates the two. They exclude each other. There can be no compromise. God and the devil cannot establish a truce. Within Christianity the importance of the Christ is that He and He alone in the awfulness of the Crucifixion met evil on its own terms and defeated it. Total warfare—a struggle involving complete elimination of one or the other—is the only possible relationship between good and evil. Redemption involves destruction of evil.

Polar duality is vastly different. The negative and the positive terminals of an electric cell are an excellent example. Without a negative and a positive there is no electricity. They oppose each other. They accept each other. There is always disquiet in the notion of a simple monism. Perhaps this explains the emotionalism of Parmenides, which required that he express his philosophy in a poem. Nonbeing cannot be—it is an absurd idea; yet Parmenides must have known he could not do without it. Nonbeing cannot be—but being cannot be either, save in the presence of nonbeing. The followers of Heraclitus always get the better of the followers of Parmenides, and the more Zenoes who arise to defend the master, the worse the situation gets. Being can be only in the context of nonbeing, and nonbeing can be only in the context of being. One without the other is like a "line" with only one terminus. No wonder the ancient Greeks preferred circles and ellipses to straight lines. No wonder Christians have had difficulty with the notion of one directional immortality, i.e., of a soul with a beginning but without an ending.

Once one starts looking for polarities in the life of the Hindus there seems to be no end of examples: twice-born and once-born, Pandavas and Kauravas, pure and impure, Holi as the festival period celebrating human equalities to balance the rest of the year with its emphasis on human inequalities, *līlā* as God's game of hide-and-seek. The combining of opposites in the lives of Hindus is so common that a contemporary Indian philosopher in a recent book refers in a single paragraph without comment to Śaṅkara's "detachment from the concerns of the world" and "his dedication to the task of social reformation." Gandhi's understanding of Hinduism had an interesting ethical polarity. He said in the *Harijan*, January 1, 1937, that after much thought he had come to the conclusion that the whole of Hinduism is found in *Īśa Upaniṣad* 1. 1, and he translated it: "All that we see in this great Universe is pervaded by God. Renounce it! Enjoy it!" Gandhi liked to describe himself in contradictory terms; e.g., in *Young India*, August 3, 1924, he said, "I am both an idolater and an iconoclast." Although Gandhi usually eschewed metaphysics, he appears to have thought polarly in this realm. He wrote as follows in *Young India*, January 21, 1926: "I am an *advaitist* and yet I can support *dvaitism*. The world is changing every moment, and is therefore unreal, it has no permanent existence. But though it is constantly changing, it has a something about it which persists and is therefore to that extent real. I have therefore no objection to calling it real and unreal."

The polarity principle is now being recognized in the methodology of modern theoretical physics. As one modern physicist has said, "We can make no progress at all in rational analysis, unless we narrow the scope of our attention, by deliberately drawing boundaries around the problem."[15] However, this methodology creates a closed system, a system with an impenetrable boundary. And this is exactly what the modern physicist is beginning to question. Is there an unbridgeable gap between the objective and the subjective, between observation and interpretation, between fact and theory? As Vajk writes, "Some of the most profound questions in modern, theoretical physics are centered on the issue of where to draw this boundary between experiment and experimenter, and when and if the two are separable from each other."[6]

I have been calling attention to the Hindu conceptions of time and polarity because I believe that such conceptions incorporated into Western culture may have meliorative effects. I can see these conceptions resulting in less emphasis on success, progress, competing, winning, breaking speed records, and getting there first—and in more emphasis on the journey than on the arrival, on the quality of life than on its length, on doing rather than accomplishing, and on craftsmanship rather than production. Today many in the West are making steps in this direction as they discover the satisfactions of working with their hands, of living close to the world of plants and animals, of engaging in noncompetitive sports, and of working with others in a spirit of love and respect. These, I believe, are marks of a new concern for the quality of life. In 1975 in Morristown, New Jersey, when the courts were deciding whether the machine which was keeping Karen Ann Quinlan alive could be turned off, one of the lawyers said, "When the quality of life replaces the sanctity of life, I fear evil has a beginning." I do not know what he intended by contrasting the quality of life and the sanctity of life. I would locate life's sanctity in its quality. Evil begins when we are not primarily concerned about the quality of life.

If we can incorporate some aspects of polarity into our ways of thinking and acting, the result will be less emphasis on competition, conflict, struggle, and the putting down of people—and more emphasis on the fun of being different, on a tolerance which rejoices in our pluralism, and on harmonious relations of peoples with alternative points of view. The total impact might be a new appreciation of the simple joys of life, a discovery of how to live fully as human beings without polluting, and finally destroying, the balance which has brought into existence the remarkable self-knowing animal which we are. We must constantly remind ourselves that there are two facets about the universe which the sciences and the theologies may not be able to explain, but certainly cannot deny:

1. Life has appeared in the universe.
2. One living form has developed self-consciousness.

As self-knowers we are self-determiners. We decide our own living arrangements. This we call our culture. To fail to take advantage of our potentialities for self-knowing and self-determining is to settle for the demonic rather than for the human. I say "demonic" rather than "animal," for the human being, despite the expressed wishes of romantics like Rousseau and Walt Whitman, cannot return to the animal. To be human means to be concerned for the meaning of human being. Nature determines that we eat, drink, sleep, and procreate; but we determine the manner of our eating, drinking, sleeping, and procreating. We are shapers of ourselves. We are Prometheus, the culture-creator. Benjamin Franklin said man is

149

homo faber, the toolmaking animal. But we make more than tools. We also make traditions of knowledge, world views, technologies, mores, social orders, means of communication, and religions. We are both the producers and the product of our culture We are both *homo hominatus* (man as made by man) and *homo hominans* (man as maker of man). The lower animals are complete animals. Their culture is instinctive. Most of them are phylo-genetically senile; that is, they are incapable of further evolution. But we are incomplete animals. We must complete ourselves. As Kierkegaard said, we cannot accept ourselves as given. We must consciously take over and "choose" ourselves. Ths is why we become so confused when we try to talk about "human nature" or "the nature of man." Such terminology suggests a false completeness. But human nature is always a *not yet*. Human nature is always in the making. Each chooses one's nature. One's nature is indeed the act of choosing. We usually choose within the limits of our own culture. I am contending that we in the West can no longer find the conceptual tools and techniques we need in Western culture.

What differences would the adaptation of the Hindu insights of cyclical time and nondestroying dualities make? It would perhaps mean a shift from the linear teleological models of human history to helenioid models, assuming that a three-dimensional helix is a compromise between a two-dimensional circle and a one-dimensional line. It would probably mean a shift from emphasis on the ideal of progress to the ideal of process; for as Nietzsche once said, man is a way, not a goal. It would probably mean relief from the pressures inherent in paradigms such as "the perfect man" and "the ideal commonwealth," and the attainment of the quiet satisfactions of rhythm, balance, harmony, and complement. It would probably mean healthier, happier, and more satisfying life-styles for the self-knowing and self-determining beings which we are. It could be the first sound step toward a universal humanity.

NOTES

1. *Odes*, 3. 6.
2. *Who is Man?* (Stanford: Stanford University Press, 1965), p. 13.
3. *Ibid.*, p. 26.

4. Harmondsworth: Penguin Books, (1977), p. 14.
5. *Ibid.*, p. 18.
6. *Ibid.*, p. 25.
7. *Ibid.*
8. *Ibid.*
9. *Ibid.*, p. 93.
10. *Ibid.*
11. *Ibid.*, p. 174.
12. *Quaestiones naturales* 3. 29. 30.
13. Ecclesiastes 1:19.
14. *De Principlis* 2. 3. 4.
15. J. Peter Vajk, *Doomsday Has Been Cancelled.* (Culver City, California: Peace Press, 1978), p. 44.
16. *Ibid.*

12. Three Platonic Silences

A philosophical malady of which we are all aware—and one which many of us suffer—is logorrhea. Yet a few philosophes have recognized the worth of silence. Charles Morris once told me that his lifelong study of semiotics had resulted in two values: (1) knowing how to use words, (2) knowing when to stop talking. One of the sermons of the Buddha recounted in the Suttas is "The Flower Sermon." This is a sermon without words. The Buddha stood before the sangha holding a flower in his hand. When one of the monks smiled and nodded in understanding, the Buddha handed him the flower, and walked out of the room. The tradition of silence is preserved in Zen Buddhism. One of the mondos recounts an occasion in which a master asked a student what he would do in a certain situation. The student placed his sandals on his head and walked away. The master cheered this as the proper response. Another person noted for his silence was Thomas Aquinas. When he first came to the University of Paris, he was nicknamed "The Dumb Ox" because of his silences. But his better known silence was the result of an experience he had at Mass on the feast of St. Nicholas in the year 1273. Josef Pieper writes, ". . . as Thomas turned back to his work after Holy Mass, he was strangely altered. He remained steadily silent; he did not write; he dictated nothing. He laid aside the *Summa Theologica* on which he had been working. . . . Reginald, his friend, asks him, troubled: 'Father, how can you want to stop such a great work?', Thomas answers only, 'I can write no more.' "[1]

In 1980 the Indiana University Press published a book by Bernard P. Dauenhauer entitled *Silence*. The subtitle is "The Phenomenon and Its Ontological Significance," and the following sentence appears in the advertisement: "The synthesis which emeges demonstrates the complexity of silence and its important role in a broadly conceived philosophy of language." This essay on Plato's silences is a modest contribution to the dialogue.

152

There are some interesting silences in the Platonic dialogues. Alcibiades reports that once at Potidaea Socrates stood quietly for twenty-four hours trying to think through a problem.[2] Plato records in the *Symposium* that Socrates has a fit of abstraction on the way to the banquet. When Agathon learns that Socrates is standing on the porch of a neighbor, he asks that a servant bring him to the banquet. But Aristodemus says, "Let him alone. He has a way of stopping anywhere and losing himself without any reason."[3]

In this chapter I wish to call attention to three Platonic, rather than Socratic, silences. The first is in *The Republic*, Book VI. In the previous book Socrates assures Glaucon and Adeimantus that the perfect state cannot become a reality until power and wisdom are integrated: "Until philosophers are kings, or the kings and princes of this world have the spirit and power of philosophy."[4] In Book VI the brothers ask, "Who is the philosopher?" Socrates replies that the philosopher is one who seeks the highest kind of knowledge. "And what is this highest kind of knowledge?" asks Adeimantus. "Is it higher than the knowledge of justice and the other virtues?" Socrates reminds Adeimantus that he has often told him that the highest knowledge is the knowledge of the Good. When Socrates is pressed to define the Good, he dodges, saying that he can give only an opinion—"And all opinions are bad." At this point Glaucon enters the discussion. He observes that Socrates is turning away just when they are in sight of the goal. Socrates relents, "Let us not at present ask what is the actual nature of the Good." He suggests as an analogical substitute that they consider "the child of the Good." Glaucon agrees, "By all means tell us about the child, and you shall remain in our debt for the account of the father."[5] But Socrates is silent about the father. In the *Timaeus* there is another use of the father symbol: "To discover the . . . Father of this whole is a hard task, and when one has found him he cannot tell of him to all."[6] Here also he does not tell about the "Father"—he does not pay the debt. Or maybe he does. Could his death as a martyr to philosophy be his payment of the debt? The word *debt* was the last word on his lips: "Crito, I owe a debt to Asclepius; will you remember to pay the debt?"[7]

At the close of the myth of the sun—"the child of the Good"— Socrates steps outside the myth, and says, "*Ouk ousias ontos tou agathou eti epekeina tēs ousias presbeia kai dunamis eperechontos.*"[8] Jowett translates

153

this as "The good is not essence, but far extends essence in dignity and power." Cornford translates it: "Goodness is not the same thing as being, but beyond being, surpassing it in dignity and power." Rouse puts it: "The good is not itself a state of knowledge but something transcending far beyond it in dignity and power." A very literal translation would be this: "The reality of the Good is not existence, rather the Good is on the yonder side of existence, standing out alone in rank and power." The Good, then, is not an object of knowledge—and so not an object of speech. Speech is required, although speech is an inadequate method for communicating about the Good. The Good must in the last analysis be demonstrated in the quality of one's life and death.

The second Platonic silence is in *The Republic*, Book 7. Plato is describing the system of education by which the ideal state selects its guardians. The education progresses through music and gymnastics, arithmetic, geometry, astronomy, and harmonics. When the candidate is thirty, a series of examinations determines who is qualified for the final study when the student "grasps by thought the real nature of good itself."[9] He has arrived "at the very end of the world of thought."[10] This period of study between ages thirty and thirty-five is devoted to dialectics. "What is dialectics?" interrupts Glaucon. Socrates replies, "You will not be able to follow me further."[11] He says he would be glad were he able to give Glaucon and Adeimantus "the truth" rather than "an image," but he will have to stay with images like the previous images of the sun, the line, and the cave. He adds that the power of discussion can show the nature of dialectics only to those who have experienced the studies just described. Plato thus indicates that silence is proper. Yet he speaks. This, which we can oxymoronically call "spoken silence," is the use of words to suggest that which transcends the meaning of words. (A few weeks ago I saw a book described in this manner: "Like great poetry, it goes well beyond words.") It is a process by which hypotheses which are necessary for communication are destroyed to get to the reality behind that which hypotheses denote. Dialectics seeks an exact account of real being. But he who knows does not speak, and he who speaks does not know. Dialectics distinguishes the Good from the things without which the Good in the Great Chain of Being cannot be nor be known. Words at best can only prepare the way for the experience of the Good.

A record of a third Platonic silence appears in the *Seventh Letter*. In fact a double silence is recorded: (1) Plato in teaching Dionysius the younger "did not explain everything,"[12] and (2) he refrained from putting into writing some of the teaching which he did orally. Dionysius has attempted to put this unwritten teaching into written form, and "certain others also have written on these same matters."[13] But, says Plato, "There is no writing of mine about these matters, nor will there ever be one."[14] He adds that if these topics can be expounded in books or in public lectures, they had best come from himself. The knowledge which Dionysius and "certain others" put into writing is "not something that can be put into words like other sciences; but after long-continued intercourse between teacher and pupil, in joint pursuit of the subject, suddenly, like light flashing forth when a fire is kindled, . . . is born in the soul and straightway nourishes itelf."[15]

What was the subject matter about which Plato was silent? Glenn Morrow says that the ultimate principles to which Plato refers are "more ultimate even than the Ideas," and speculates that it may have been the One and the Indefinite Dyad.[16] I do not think we need to speculate as to the subject matter, for we are informed in *The Republic*, 509C that the Good is transcendent to being and knowing. The Good is not a Form, not even a Form of Forms. It is the ground of all Forms, the principle of being, the *archē* of *ousia*, the *principle* of knowledge—not an object of knowledge, and the *principle* of value—not a value. The Good was the subject matter Plato taught Dionysius in his opportunity to fashion a philosopher king. I find it unprofitable to assume Plato had two doctrines—an exoteric and an acromatic, and to speculate as to the content of the acromatic. I take the distinction between exoteric and acromatic to be more a distinction of methods of instruction than of contents of instruction.

The *Seventh Letter* is a defense of Plato's pedagogical methods. The order of being, knowing, and valuing is *down* the Divided Line from Forms to images, but the order of learning is *up* the Divided Line from images to Forms. When Socrates says that "we place dialectics on top of our other studies like a coping stone,"[17] he is speaking correctly in the order of learning—it is *placed* there by the learner—but this is not correct in the order of being—it *is* there. Ontologically, epistemologically, and axiologically the Divided Line is like a rope ladder—securely attached at the top; pedagogically the Divided Line is like a wooden ladder—anchored at the bottom.

The three instruments of knowing, says Plato, are words, definitions, and diagrams. Each is inadequate to its task. Words are arbitrarily chosen: "their names are by no means fixed . . . there is no reason why what we call 'circles' might not be called 'straight lines,' and the straight lines 'circles.' "[18] The same can be said of definitions: "there is nothing fixed about it."[19] As for diagrams, Plato says, "Every circle that we make or draw in common life is full of characteristics that contradict the 'fifth,' for it everywhere touches a straight line, while the circle itself, we say, has in it not the slightest element belonging to a contrary nature."[20] These three instruments of knowing must be used by a living teacher in a one-to-one relationship with a pupil to modify, alter, interpret, or translate the meaning of words, definitions, and diagrams so they become understood by the pupil. The elements brought into play in the teaching process—*epistēmē* (knowledge), *nous* (reason) and *alēthēs doxa* (right opinion) are the elements of knowing as the subjective apprehension, for, as Plato says, they are "in our minds, not in words or bodily shapes."[21] It is interesting to note that these three elements of learning, which are referred to as "the fourth," constitute the epistemological side of the Divided Line as presented in *The Republic*. The three instruments of knowing, which Plato calls "the three things," and the subjective apprehension, which he calls "the fourth," lead to the proper conclusion of discursive reasoning. This conclusion he calls *poion ti* ("the somewhat"), *to poion ti* ("the particular property"), and *gnōston* ("the knowable"). The "somewhat" is the region of vagueness and obscurity, the region of sense perception and practical life. It is often the only result of inquiries.

But beyond the region of the "somewhat" is the region of the "what" (*ti*). The discovery of the "what" transcends the fourth. It is reached only by means of "a leaping spark," "a light flashing forth," "an illumination." The term used—*eklampsis*—comes from the verb *eklampō* meaning to shine forth or to light up. The tutor uses words, definitions, and diagrams to stimulate the student to right opinion, to reason, and to knowledge, but unless there is an *eklampsis* the student may not reach the "what." In addition to *ti* as a denotation for "the fifth" Plato uses *to on* (the being of an object), *to ti* (the real essence), and *alēthōs on* (the truly real). The "somewhat" is the conclusion reached by valid rational reasoning; the "what" is not necessarily the object of mystical contemplation inasmuch as it is preceded by the normal rational methods. But in addition to the rational subjective apprehension there must be an "affinity with the object."[22] There are no short cuts. It is not logical, nor illogical, but perhaps translogical.[23]

There is a passage in Augustine's *Confessions* which summarizes his own theory in a manner very similar to Plato's account in the *Seventh Letter*: "And thus, by degrees, I passed from bodies to the soul, which makes use of the senses of the body to perceive; and thence to its inward faculty, to which the bodily senses represent outward things. [Cf. Aristotle's *sensus communis*.] . . . and thence, again, I passed on to the reasoning faculty, to which whatever is received from the senses of the body is referred to be judged, which also, finding itself to be variable in me, raised itself up to its own intelligence, and from habit drew away my thoughts, withdrawing itself from the crowds of contradictory phantasms; that so it might find out that light by which it was besprinkled, when, without all doubting, it cried out, that the unchangeable was to be preferred before the changeable; whence also it knew that unchangeable, which, unless it had in some way known, it could have had no sure ground for preferring it to the changeable. And thus, with the flash of a trembling glance, it arrived at that which is."[24]

Not all philosophers welcome the leaping spark. Lovejoy calls it an example of "the pathos of the esoteric." He writes, "How exciting and how welcome is the sense of initiation into hidden mysteries! And how effectively have certain philosophers—notably Schelling and Hegel a century ago, and Bergson in our own generation— satisfied the human craving for this experience, by representing the central insight of their philosophy as a thing to be reached, not through a consecutive progress of thought guided by the ordinary logic available to every man, but through a sudden leap whereby one rises to a place of insight wholly different in its principles from the level of the mere understanding."[25]

157

An excellent example of *eklampsis* comes to us from modern physics. Consider, for example, the view that light is both wave and particle, or that atomic physicists can determine velocity or position within the atom but not both. Robert Marsh writes, "The normal reaction to a first exposure to relativity is: 'I think I understand it; I just don't believe it.' Normally it takes a physicist about five years of contact with the ideas before he feels comfortable with them—not because they are complex or obscure, but just terribly strange. . . . The reader is implored to have faith, in the hope that all will turn out self-consistent in the end."[26] Robert Oppenheimer says that the physicist must learn to understand that the electron is neither at rest nor in motion.[27]

Plato admits there are "kinship and similarity"[28] between *nous* and "the fifth," yet he holds that one does not move easily to "the fifth" as one does from "the third" and "the fourth" to the "somewhat." The movement from "the fourth" to "the fifth" is made in a jump which defies rational analysis. Plato says that "it is brought to birth in the soul on a sudden;"[29] "it is as light that is kindled by a leaping spark;"[30] and it "nourishes itself"[31] once it has become a reality. The student must discover the truth for himself.

I submit that *eklampsis* is that which distinguishes the Platonic and the Aristotelian theories of knowledge. The "somewhat," the Gestalt of attributes, is, for Aristotle, the object of knowing. We might say that this sort of knowing is that which we test in true-false examinations. The other sort of knowing is that which was evidenced one day in one of my undergraduate classes when a brilliant freshman, after about a month of trying to understand Whitehead's theory of prehensions, jumped from his seat and shouted, "I've got it!" I believe that there is a parallel to *eklampsis* in Aristotle, and, as might be expected, it is in the area of perception rather than conception. Corresponding to Plato's distinction between "the what" and "the somewhat" in the order of knowing is Aristotle's distinction between "the suchness of something" (*tou toioude*) and "the thisness of something" (*toude tinos*) in the order of sensing.

A key passage is *Posterior Analytics* 87 b 27-29, which Mure translates as "Scientific knowledge is not possible through the act of perception. Even if perception as a faculty is of 'the such' and not merely of a 'this somewhat,' yet one must at any rate actually

perceive a 'this somewhat,' and at a definite place and time." I offer
as a literal translation: "It is impossible to know universals through
direct perception. For even if there is a perceiving of the suchness of
something and not of the thisness of something, still it is necessary to
perceive this something whether in suchness form or in thisness form
as located in a this-here context." What Aristotle is saying is that the
preanalytic sense datum is always a *ti kai pou kai nun* (a this which is
both here and now). This raw unanalyzed datum may be interpreted
in either of two ways: (1) as a *tou toi oude* (a such-like sort of thing),
i.e., as a class of particulars of which "this here and now" is a
particular instance—*a such*; (2) or as a *toude tinos* (a this somewhat),
i.e., as a particular with all its unique features—a mere this. Aristotle
is affirming his view that scientific knowledge—the knowledge of
universals—is not possible through the simple act of sensation. One
may regard sensing as the being aware of the generic through the
awareness of a particular, e.g., one might look at a red book and say
that one is seeing red rather than that one is seeing a particular shade
of red spread out in specific dimensions and with unique features, yet
one cannot deny that what one is actually aware of is this particular
red. The universal is never sensed as universal, since universals *qua*
universals are not located in one place and one time. Therefore, one
must engage in an *aphairesis* (a taking away, or an abstracting) by
which one removes the "this here and now" character of the sense
datum and perceives it as "the suchness of something" rather than
"the thisness of something," as red rather than as a unique shade of
red. Aristotle's leap is from "thisness" to "suchness," from the
particular to the universal; Plato's from "the fourth" to "the fifth,"
from the subjective apprehension not to the merely knowable but to
the very being. The Good as the integral ground of being-knowing-
valuing cannot be grasped by step-by- step discursive reasoning. The
illumination has all the immediacy of a leaping spark. For Aristotle
the leap is a movement of ordinary people, and it can be described in
ordinary language. For Plato the leap is made by "golden youth,"
only "after long-continued intercourse between teacher and pupil, in
joint pursuit of the subject."[32] The account of the teaching of Dionysius is available only because the tyrant broke faith with his
teacher in writing an interpretation of the instruction and the experience. Plato rebukes his former pupil, but he tells us very little about

the illumination experience and its object. They remain something that cannot be put into words.

The three Platonic silences can be stated in capsule form:

1. The first silence refers to a reality/value which must be exemplified in one's life and death.
2. The second silence refers to an experience which transcends words.
3. The third silence refers to a translogical leap in thought.

NOTES

1. _The Silence of St. Thomas._ (Chicago: Regnery, 1957), p. 39.
2. _Symposium_ 220.
3. _Ibid.,_ 175.
4. _Republic_ 473.
5. _Ibid.,_ 506.
6. _Timaeus_ 28.
7. _Phaedo_ 118.
8. _Republic_ 509.
9. _Ibid.,_ 532.
10. _Ibid._
11. _Ibid.,_ 533.
12. _Seventh Letter_ 341. All quotations are from the translation of Glenn Morrow unless otherwise noted.
13. _Ibid._
14. _Ibid._
15. _Ibid._
16. _Plato's Epistles._ (New York: Bobbs-Merrill Co., 1962), pp. 66-67.
17. _Republic_ 534. W. H. D. Rouse translation.
18. _Seventh Letter_ 343.
19. _Ibid._
20. _Ibid._
21. _Ibid._
22. _Ibid.,_ 344. R. G. Bury translation.
23. A modern Indian philosopher writes as follows about the knowing of Brahman: "The intuition of Brahman transcends the limits of the logical intellect, though it is the fulfilment of logical thinking." P.N. Srinivasachari, _The Philosophy of Visishtadvaita._ (Adyar, Madras: The Theosophical Publishing House, 1946), p. xxxvii.
24. 7. 17. Tr. by J. G. Pilkington.
25. Arthur O. Lovejoy, _The Great Chain of Being._ 14th printing. (Cambridge: Harvard University Press, 1978), pp. 11-12.

26. Robert Marsh, *Physics for Poets*. (New York: McGraw-Hill, 1970), p. 128.
27. See Huston Smith, *Forgotten Truth* (New York: Harper & Row, 1976), p. 107.
28. *Seventh Letter* 342. Bury translation.
29. *Ibid.*, 341.
30. *Ibid.*
31. *Ibid.*
32. *Ibid.*

Postscript

Lord Śiva has three eyes, the right one is the sun, the left the moon, and in the middle of the forehead fire. The third eye is said to be the eye of destruction. But fire purges as well as destroys. The Tamil Śaivite poet Māṇikka Vāsahar sang,

> He shew'd the path of love, that so
> Fruit of past deeds might ended be.
> Cleansed my mind so foul,
> He made me like a god.[1]

The name *Śiva* means *auspicious*. And so he is in his five functions of making, preserving, destroying, judging, and purifying.

The hope of the author of these essays is that readers will find them constructive rather than destructive. Our world has many cynics and detractors. *Third Eye Philosophy* is designed as a contribution to critical philosophy in the mathematical sense of the term *critical*, i.e., a point at which a change takes place.

NOTE

1. Māṇikya Vāchaka (whose name has been Tamilized to Māṇikka Vāsahar) lived in the ninth or tenth century A.D. He was one of the saints of South India known as Aḍiyars or Nāyanārs. His work is titled the *Tiruyāchakam* (Sacred Utterance). The portion of the poem quoted comes from *Hymns of the Tamil Śaivite Saints*, translated and edited by F. Kingsbury and G. E. Phillips. Calcutta: Association Press, 1921, p. 127.